Paganism for Beginners

Unlocking Norse Magic, Druidry, Celtic Shamanism, Runes, Signs, and Symbols

Free Bonus from Silvia Hill available for limited time

Hi Spirituality Lovers!

My name is Silvia Hill, and first off, I want to THANK YOU for reading my book.

Now you have a chance to join my exclusive spirituality email list so you can get the ebooks below for free as well as the potential to get more spirituality ebooks for free! Simply click the link below to join.

P.S. Remember that it's 100% free to join the list.

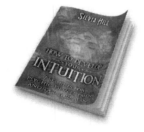

🙌 9 Types of Spirit Guides and How to Connect to Them

🙌 How to Develop Your Intuition: 7 Secrets for Psychic Development and Tarot Reading

🙌 Tarot Reading Secrets for Love, Career, and General Messages

Access your free bonuses here
https://livetolearn.lpages.co/paganism-for-beginners-paperback/

Table of Contents

Introduction

Most people think of Paganism as a single religion based on ancient healing traditions and reverence towards nature and polytheism. While it's true that both ancient and contemporary Pagan practices involve elements of healing, spirituality, nature, and the divine, there are many different approaches through which this is done. Even in ancient times, the number of Pagan religions was vast - and this was before they started to incorporate elements from other, more dominant religions like Christianity. In modern times, there is no limit to what you can incorporate into your practices. It's all about what feels right for you based on your cultural and religious background.

Polytheism and pantheism are still traditionally present in contemporary Pagan practices, as both beliefs allow for immense diversity. Whether you wish to honor one deity or several, it's totally up to you. Unlike in many other religions, female deities have just as distinguished roles as their male counterparts - and in some traditions, even more important ones.

Another factor that puts modern Pagan traditions apart from other religions and even ancient traditions is the choice of solitary practice. In ancient times, lone practitioners were rare to find. However, nowadays, due to the diversity of traditions, many people feel safe and confident learning the Pagan ways on their own. Whether you go down this path or want to join a coven, a group, or any other Pagan community, you'll have plenty of support from fellow practitioners.

Despite having different approaches, the names of some modern practices like Paganism and Wicca are used interchangeably. Wicca is one of the most popular Pagan practices nowadays - mainly because it's also the newest. This book will clarify all the differences between these two practices and lead you to the magical path of practical Wicca.

Other Pagan practices, such as Norse Paganism, can be just as inspiring. It's enough to delve into the tales of Nordic mythology to see how much these practices meant to the old Norse people. From guiding them through battles to protection during the harsh winters, Norse people relied on their gods and ancestors for everything. Their most common practice - runic divination- is still in use today. With the help of the information you'll receive in this book and enough spiritual dedication, you can learn this magical art too.

Another popular form of gathering wisdom in Norse Paganism was journeying. This was typically performed by shamans, who used the information they accessed for healing - whether physical, mental, or spiritual. However, as you'll learn from the book, Shamanism was also present in other Celtic Pagan approaches. Celtic Shamanism incorporates some of the most complex traditions, with some of them taking rigorous practice to master.

The book will also introduce you to Druidry - a practice shrouded in mysticism and only taught to selected members of society. In ancient times, Druids were the most (and sometimes only) educated members of Celtic tribes who recorded the tribe's history. While there are many ways to become a Druid, there are still plenty of mysteries around this practice. The lack of written evidence on ancient Druidry caused modern traditions to be loosely based on its ancestor.

Chapter 1: A Brief History of Paganism

Paganism is one of the oldest spiritual traditions in the world. It dates back to prehistoric times and can be found in many different cultures around the globe. Paganism is an umbrella term used to describe various earth-based spiritual traditions. It generally refers to a nature-based religion that worships and respects the earth and its creatures. It is often seen as a more ancient or primal form of religion, one that is closer to the natural world. Pagans believe that the divine can be found in all things and often look to nature for guidance and inspiration. Pagans often practice their faith through rituals and ceremonies that honor the earth and all its elements.

Paganism is one of the oldest spiritual traditions in the world.
https://www.pexels.com/photo/bottles-on-black-round-table-in-the-room-with-fireplace-and-cow-skull-7190305/

Paganism dates back thousands of years, and its origins can be traced back to some of the earliest known civilizations. Over the centuries, it has evolved and changed to reflect the cultures and beliefs of its practitioners. Today, there are many different forms of Paganism practiced all over the world.

The Origin of Paganism

Paganism is thought to have originated in the Stone Age with the early hunter-gatherer societies. This was the time when humans first began to form organized religions. Pagan beliefs and practices likely developed out of a need to explain the natural world and our place within it. As early humans began to domesticate plants and animals, they likely also began to develop a belief in animism, the idea that all living things have a spirit. This belief helped early humans to form a connection with the natural world and to understand its place within it. Pagan beliefs likely developed in small, tight-knit communities where everyone knew and trusted one another. As these communities grew more extensive and more complex, they began to develop organized religions.

Pagan beliefs likely first developed in Europe and Asia, as these were the regions where humans began forming organized religions. However, Paganism can be found in almost every culture across the globe.

Paganism can be traced back to various ancient cultures, such as the Celts, Greeks, and Romans. However, during the Middle Ages, Paganism began to take hold in Europe. This was due mainly to the Christianization of the continent. Christianity began to replace many of the older Pagan traditions. Still, some people continued to practice their Pagan beliefs in secret. This often led to persecution from the Church. In some cases, Pagans were even put to death for their beliefs.

Despite centuries of persecution, Paganism has survived and even thrived in many parts of the world. Today, there are an estimated two million Pagans worldwide.

Etymology

Paganism has its roots in pre-Christian, indigenous beliefs from around the world. The word "pagan" is derived from Latin and was likely used as a derogatory term by early Christians to describe those who continued to practice their Pagan beliefs. Over time, the term has been reclaimed by many Pagans and is now used proudly to describe themselves.

It was first used to describe people who did not follow the major world religions, such as Christianity, Judaism, and Islam. Over time, the word came to be associated with any religion that was not Christian.

It was widely practiced all over Europe, but with the rise of Christianity in the 4th century, it started declining. However, it was still practiced until the 10th century to some extent. In the 1500s, the Renaissance was a period of intense interest in classical culture; Paganism was incorporated into Europe's arts, music, literature, and ethics during this time.

Paganism began to re-emerge as a distinct religious movement in the 20th century. In the United Kingdom, the Pagan Federation was founded in 1971 to support Pagans of all traditions. Since then, the movement has grown steadily throughout the world.

Paganism is an umbrella term that covers a wide range of spiritual and religious beliefs. Some people use the term to describe their spirituality, while others refer to organized religions like Wicca, Druidry, and Heathenry.

What Is Paganism?

Paganism is a diverse and decentralized religious movement that centers on worshipping nature gods and goddesses. Pagans often celebrate their beliefs through rituals and festivals that honor the changing seasons and life cycles. Many Pagans also choose to live in harmony with the natural world, working to protect the environment from harm.

Paganism is not a single religion but a collection of different spiritual traditions. Some worship a specific god or goddess, while others focus on a group of deities.

Pagans also believe in magical and supernatural powers and benefit from spells and charms in their daily lives. Paganism has no central authority or figurehead, and there is no one set of beliefs or practices that all practitioners follow. Instead, each Pagan chooses what to believe and how to worship.

Pagan Gods

Paganism is a polytheistic religion that believes in multiple gods and goddesses. Each god or goddess represents a different aspect of the natural world or human experience. For example, there might be a god of the sun, a god of love, or a goddess of wisdom. Pagans also believe in magic and the power of nature.

Thor, Odin, Freyja, Frigg, Freyr, Tyr, Loki, and Heimall are the most well-known Norse deities. However, there were many lesser-known gods and goddesses. The pantheon of the Greek Olympians includes Zeus, Poseidon, Hades, Aphrodite, Hermes, and a host of other deities. Every aspect of human experience was attributed to one or more of these gods and goddesses.

Pagan Symbols

There are many misconceptions about Paganism, such as the idea that pagans worship the devil or that they are all witches. That is not accurate. Pagans do not believe in the devil, and not all of them are witches.

Some popular pagan symbols include the pentacle (a five-pointed star), the Celtic cross, the triple goddess, and the horned god. These symbols are often used in rituals, ceremonies, and everyday life. They are worn as jewelry, displayed on walls or altars, or carried in pockets or bags.

Paganism puts great stress on nature and the earth. It is often considered a form of animism, which is the belief that everything, including animals, plants, and rocks, has a spirit.

In the Egyptian pantheon, Isis and Osiris were the most popular gods. Isis was the goddess of motherhood and nature, while Osiris was the god of the underworld and the afterlife. Other popular Egyptian deities include Ra, the sun god, and Hathor, the goddess of love and beauty. The Roman pantheon includes Jupiter, the king of the gods, and Juno, the goddess of marriage and motherhood.

Pagan Beliefs and Rituals

Pagans believe in magic, reincarnation, karma, and the power of nature. Their rituals and celebrations are often based on the changing of the seasons and the cycles of nature. The most well-known Pagan festival is Beltane, celebrated on May 1st. Other popular Pagan festivals include Samhain (pronounced "sow-in"), celebrated on October 31st, and Imbolc, celebrated on February 2nd.

You'll find more information on the different beliefs and practices among different Pagan traditions later in this book. For now, let's take a closer look at the history of Paganism.

Paganism in Europe

European Paganism is a rich and varied belief system rooted in the ancient world. From the Celts to the Norse, pagans have long been associated with nature worship, magic, and deep respect for the natural world.

Pre-Christian Europe was a very different place than it is today. The land was mostly forest, and people lived in small villages or tribes. They were farmers or herders and worshipped gods and goddesses related to nature. There were many different tribes, each one with unique customs and beliefs.

When the Romans conquered Europe, they brought their religion, Christianity, with them. Christian missionaries tried to convert the pagans, but many held on to their old beliefs. Christianity gradually became the dominant religion, but Paganism never entirely died out. In the Middle Ages, there was a revival of Paganism in Europe, which has continued to grow.

Paganism in England

England has a long history of Paganism, dating back to the Bronze Age. The most well-known pagan deity in England is the goddess Brigid, the Lady of the Lake. She is associated with fire, healing, and poetry. Another popular deity is the Horned God, associated with hunting and animals.

The native tribes of England worshipped various gods and goddesses, including the god of the sun, the god of the moon, and the goddess of fertility. Paganism was the dominant religion in England until the arrival of Christianity in the 7th century.

Paganism declined during the 10th and 11th centuries as the Christian church became more powerful. By the 13th century, it had all but disappeared from England. However, it experienced a resurgence in the 18th and 19th centuries when people began to explore other religions.

Paganism in America

American Paganism has a long and complicated history. It is difficult to say precisely when or how Paganism first arrived on the shores of the United States. Some Pagans believe that the ancient indigenous peoples of North and South America practiced a form of it, while others believe that the first Pagans in America were European immigrants who brought their own beliefs and practices with them.

European colonists brought various pagan traditions, including Druidry, Celtic Shamanism, Norse Magic, and Wicca, to the Americas. These traditions mixed and mingled with each other and the native beliefs already present in America, creating a rich and diverse Pagan tradition.

Paganism continued to grow in popularity throughout the 19th and 20th centuries. In the 1960s and 1970s, the feminist and civil rights movements sparked a renewed interest in Paganism and other alternative spiritualities. In the late 20th century, Paganism began to regain popularity in America. This resurgence was partly due to the growing awareness of environmental issues and the popularity of books and movies that featured pagan characters (such as The Lord of the Rings and Harry Potter).

Today, there are an estimated 1 million Pagans in America, and the number is increasing daily.

History of Paganism in Iceland

Paganism was the dominant religion in Iceland before the Christianization of the island in 1000 AD. It is thought that

Paganism first arrived in Iceland around 900 AD, brought by settlers from Scandinavia and the British Isles. Paganism continued to be practiced in Iceland even after Christianity became the dominant religion.

Iceland did not officially become a Christian country until 1000CE. Paganism declined in popularity after that, but some Icelanders still practiced it into the 13th century. After that, Christianity became the only religion practiced in Iceland.

The Icelandic Pagans also believed in many other beings, such as elves, dwarves, giants, and trolls. Some of these beings were thought to be helpful, while others were considered to be dangerous. Pagan beliefs and practices were passed down orally from generation to generation.

There are no written records of Paganism in Iceland, so we know about it mostly from Christian sources written after the country converted to Christianity.

Norway and Sweden

Paganism was also the dominant religion in Norway and Sweden before Christianization. The pagan religion held out longest in northern lands, Norway and Sweden.

Norway had an early start in its conversion to Christianity, with King Haakon I (ruled 934-961 C.E.) accepting that religion in the 1020s. The country was, however, slow to give up its pagan ways. It was not until the early 11th century that Christianity became firmly established in Norway.

Sweden, on the other hand, did not accept Christianity until the middle of the 11th century. King Olof Skötkonung (ruled 995-1022 C.E.) was the first Swedish ruler to be baptized in 1001 C.E., but it was not until his son, Anund Jakob (ruled 1008-1050 C.E.), that Christianity became widely accepted in Sweden.

Paganism in Asia

Paganism is also practiced in many parts of Asia. In Japan, the native religion, Shinto, is a form of Paganism. Many Pagans in China practice Taoism, an indigenous Chinese religion with elements of Paganism.

In India, there are numerous pagan traditions still practiced today. And in Korea, Shamanism is still practiced by a small minority of the population.

Paganism in Ireland

Ireland was a pagan country before the arrival of Christianity in the 5th century. Pagans in Ireland continue to practice a variety of ancient traditions. These traditions include the construction of temporary altars or shrines, the lighting of fires, and the offering of gifts to the gods and goddesses. They also celebrate various seasonal festivals, such as Beltane and Mabon.

Neo-Paganism in Ireland is a modern movement that revives ancient pagan traditions. It is practiced by a small minority of people in Ireland, most of whom are members of the Pagan Federation of Ireland. There are several different types of Neo-Paganism practiced in Ireland.

Paganism in Africa

It is often associated with ancient Egyptian religion and, more recently, with the traditional religions of the San people. However, there is no one African Pagan tradition. Instead, there are a variety of pagan traditions that are followed across the continent.

African traditions believe that ancestors maintain spiritual connections with living relatives. There is a general tendency for ancestral spirits to be kind and good. Negative actions by ancestral spirits cause minor illnesses and warn people that they have crossed the wrong path.

San people, also known as Bushmen, are indigenous people of Southern Africa. The San follow a pagan religion based on animism, the belief that everything in nature has a spirit. Ancestors are thought to be powerful spirits who can help or harm the living.

Australia and New Zealand

Paganism is also practiced in Australia and New Zealand. The most common type of Paganism in these countries is Wicca.

The pagan religion of the Māori people is known as the Māori religion. As a form of animism, it holds that everything in nature is spiritual. Māori religion teaches that humans are connected to all things in nature and that we must respect and care for the natural world.

Paganism is a growing religion in Australia. In 2016, it was estimated that there were about 27194 Pagans in Australia. This number is expected to grow in the future.

Paganism and the Indian Sub-Continent

Paganism was also practiced in the Indian subcontinent. The most common type of Paganism in the sub-continent is Hinduism. It is the oldest and most prominent religion in the sub-continent. It is a polytheistic religion, meaning Hindus believe in many gods and goddesses. There are millions of Hindus living in the sub-continent.

Paganism Today

This is a hard number to estimate because Paganism is not an organized religion like Christianity. There is no single Pagan organization or leader. Instead, Paganism is a collection of many different spiritual and religious traditions. Each tradition has its own beliefs, practices, and followers.

It is believed that there are between 1 and 4 million Pagans worldwide. Most Pagans live in the United States, followed by the United Kingdom, Canada, and Australia.

Misconception about Paganism

Paganism is often misunderstood and misrepresented by mainstream society, largely because Pagans do not have a central authority or figurehead, such as the Pope in Catholicism. As a result, Paganism is often seen as an amorphous and disorganized religion. Additionally, Paganism has no strict dogma or creed, which further contributes to its misunderstood reputation.

Paganism is also frequently associated with Satanism because both religions share similar beliefs and practices. However, Pagans do not worship Satan or any other malevolent deity. Instead, they believe in a pantheon of gods and goddesses who represent various aspects of the natural world.

Paganism is not an evil or dark religion. In fact, Pagans have a deep respect for nature and all living things. They believe that we are all connected to the earth and its elements. It is a peaceful and tolerant religion that celebrates life in all its forms.

The roots of Paganism can be traced back to the ancient civilizations of Mesopotamia, Egypt, and Greece. These cultures all believed in a pantheon of gods and goddesses who ruled over the natural world. They also shared other similarities, such as a belief in magic and the use of oracles and divination.

Types of Paganism

There are many different types of Paganism. Some of the most common types include Animism, Druidism, Wicca, Odinism, Asatru, Celtic Reconstructionism, and Heathenry. As an umbrella term, Paganism refers to various spiritual and religious beliefs. Each type has its own set of beliefs and practices.

Animism is the belief that everything in nature has a spirit. This includes animals, plants, rocks, and even inanimate objects. Animism is one of the oldest religions in the world.

Druidism is a type of Paganism that honors the gods and goddesses of Celtic mythology. Druids were the priestly class of the Celts. They were responsible for performing ceremonies, such as weddings and funerals. Druidism is a nature-based religion that emphasizes harmony with the natural world.

Wicca is a type of Paganism that worships the goddesses of nature. Wiccans believe in magic and the power of spells and rituals. Having been founded in the 1950s, Wicca is still a relatively new religion.

Odinism is a type of Paganism that revolves around worshiping the Norse gods, like Odin and Thor. Odinists believe in the power of magic and runes. They also place great importance on courage, honor, and loyalty.

Asatru is a type of Paganism that worships the Norse gods. Asatru is similar to Odinism, but it emphasizes ethics and morality more.

Celtic Reconstructionism is a type of Paganism that seeks to revive the Celtic culture and religion. Celtic Reconstructionists believe in following the old ways of their ancestors. They also place great importance on preserving the Celtic language and culture.

Heathenry is a type of Paganism that worships the Germanic gods, such as Odin and Thor. Heathens believe in magic and the power of runes. They also place great importance on courage, honor, and loyalty.

The following chapters will introduce you to some of the most common beliefs of Paganism. You'll learn about their practices. By the end of this book, you'll have a good understanding of the different types of Paganism and how they differ.

Paganism is an ancient and varied religious tradition emphasizing nature worship, personal autonomy, and individual spiritual experience. Paganism first emerged in the early days of human civilization, when people began to worship the natural world around them. This early form of religion focused on animism, or the belief that everything in nature contains a spirit.

As societies developed, Paganism evolved to include the worship of specific deities associated with different aspects of nature. This led to the rise of polytheistic pagan religions, which worship multiple gods and goddesses. Paganism also began to incorporate mystical practices like magic and divination. These elements were often seen as ways to connect with the divine or natural world.

In recent years, Paganism has experienced a resurgence in popularity, particularly in the form of Neo-Paganism. This modern pagan movement emphasizes a return to nature worship and pagan values.

Chapter 2: Pagan Beliefs and Spirituality

Paganism isn't just a belief but also a spiritual concept. Unlike many other beliefs that mainly focus on sinning, punishment, and suffering, the ancient pagans had a more positive view of the world. They regarded it as a place to live life to the fullest and experience happiness and joy. The pagans believed that the divine was always around them in everything that nature embodies. They often felt close to the divine and one with the universe, which is why nature is highly revered in Paganism.

The pagans believed that the divine was always around them in everything that nature embodies

https://www.pexels.com/photo/ornaments-and-lighted-candle-on-a-table-6154151/

This chapter will delve into Paganism as a spiritual concept and further discuss its various deities, beliefs, festivals, and the significance of nature in Paganism.

The Ancient Pagans' Beliefs

Ancient Paganism revolved around polytheism which is the belief in the existence and the worshiping of multiple deities. Unlike monotheists, who believe there is only one god who is responsible for everything, polytheists believe there is a different god for every aspect of life. The ancient pagans even believed that there were different deities for cities, forests, families, streams, and mountains.

Paganism is more flexible and welcoming than other beliefs and religions due to how inclusive polytheism is. If you look at any monotheistic religion, you'll find that they are all exclusive. For instance, Christians don't practice Judaism or go to temples, and vice versa. If one chooses to practice a religion, one must stick to it, as followers of monotheistic religions aren't allowed to practice more than one religion. The ancient pagans didn't have to follow these strict rules. Since they were polytheists, they were free to worship as many gods as they wanted. This made Paganism one of the most tolerant and diverse beliefs. Pagans believed they could worship any deity they wanted and still be accepted without any judgment.

The pagans worshiped both male and female deities, and these gods and goddesses were depicted as regular human beings. They weren't perfect. They were flawed like the rest of mankind. Yet, they were highly revered for their power and wisdom.

Although many religions believe in the afterlife and that all their actions heavily influence what their life will be like in the afterlife, pagans have a different view. They didn't concern themselves with what will happen after death and only focused on their lives instead. In fact, some pagans didn't believe in the existence of the afterlife or any similar concept to heaven and hell. However, their ancient literary works told a different story as many of their classics featured the idea of the afterlife, like in the famous poem Odyssey by Homer. This poem, and other similar literary works, were entertaining and even masterpieces, but they didn't always provide an actual portrayal of the ancient pagans' beliefs. Their remaining tombstones showed their lack of belief in the afterlife. They often inscribed Latin abbreviations on their tombstones to indicate that the deceased doesn't exist anymore. This proves that they believe the soul ceased to exist after death. As a result, some pagans didn't live their lives to please their gods. They didn't believe there was such a thing as sinning, so they didn't feel the need to atone for their mistakes, repent, or ask for salvation. They believed in being good individuals because it gave them a sense of pride and fulfillment and didn't involve the afterlife or pleasing their deities.

However, this wasn't the case for all pagans, as others firmly believed in the afterlife and lived their lives according to a set of rules in the hopes that their souls would end up in a better place after they died. For instance, the Vikings and Norse people believed in the afterlife and had a similar concept of heaven that they called Valhalla, a place where the souls of noble warriors go after they die. The ancient Greeks believed that the soul traveled to the underworld, which was ruled by the god Hades, where they would spend eternity. The ancient Egyptians also believed in the afterlife and that death wasn't the end of the soul's journey. In fact, death transitions the soul from the realm of the living to the realm of the dead. Where and how they would spend their afterlife depended on how they lived their lives. Just like some people nowadays believe that good people go to heaven while bad ones go to hell, the pagans had similar beliefs. Those who led an honorable life ended up in the Field of Reeds, their version of heaven, where good people spent their afterlife. However, if a person committed many bad deeds and lived dishonorable lives, they would be severely punished, and their soul would cease to exist.

Pagans also believed in karma, defined in the modern world as "what goes around, comes around." In other words, your actions will impact your destiny, whether good or bad. It isn't the gods or even the concept of fate that is responsible for karma; it is a law of life that many people today believe and live by. Reincarnation was another belief in ancient Paganism that was associated with karma. It is believed that when the body withers after a person dies, the soul can experience a rebirth, whether in the form of a human being, animal, or plant. What or who you come back to depends on your karma. Although few pagans believed in reincarnation, there were a number of them that accepted this belief. Some religions and beliefs don't have a favorable outlook on reincarnation; however, the pagans' view was more positive. They considered it a joyful experience where the soul could learn and grow.

Ancient Paganism and the Myth of Creation

How was the world created? This is a question that many religions and beliefs have attempted to answer, and Paganism is no different. According to many religions, there is God, and He is the one who created the universe.

While others believe that the universe was the result of the big bang theory, the answer to this question is Paganism may be tricky. There are different beliefs in Paganism, and each has its own myth of how the world came to be. However, most of the creation stories in this belief share the same elements. The first element is that before mankind came to be, there was nothing, an emptiness, and the world was chaotic and dark. This darkness was different from the normal darkness that mankind is accustomed to when the sun sets. It was the original darkness that was impossible to imagine or comprehend. It was what the world looked like before order was established. The universe was created from the void, and everything that threatened the universe's order or caused chaos was sent to the underworld. Chaos was never destroyed but remained in the background threatening to rule over the world once again.

Order usually comes out of nothing; however, each story has its own interpretation of this moment. For instance, according to ancient Greek mythology, the world came to be through birth. The void, an all-goddess called Eurynome, mated with a serpent called Ophion, who was also a void and gave birth to the universe. In ancient Egyptian mythology, the universe came to be through the God Ptah masturbating. These myths and others have in common that a certain action took place to create the universe, which is the second common element that all creation myths share.

The third element that creation myths have in common is that mankind was created in the creator's image, and the universe and all its beings represent this creator. This means that all creation is planned, and nothing is done by accident. In other words, what the deity creates is a mirror of them and their nature.

The Ancient Pagan's Deities

The ancient pagans assigned a deity for everything. This makes sense since they didn't have the methods that exist in the modern world, like technology, modern medicine, or irrigation methods. Everything seemed out of their control, so they wanted to rely on something more powerful and wiser than themselves. These deities came through where mankind failed. They made their lives easier and, in some cases, better. These deities could take away their misery and pain and provide for the people.

Now, we will look at the most significant deities in ancient Paganism.

Odin

If you are familiar with Marvel comics and the Thor movies, then the name Odin will definitely ring a bell. He was the chief deity in Norse mythology and the god of war, poetry, and wisdom. Odin lived in Valhalla and had shape-shifting abilities. He would often change his form and walk among mankind. Although Odin is often depicted as an old man with one eye, this isn't his original form. He used to have two eyes, but he exchanged one of them to gain immense wisdom. Odin had an eight-legged horse named Sleipnir that he rode over the water and across the skies.

Thor

Almost everyone is familiar with Thor, thanks to comic books that made this deity very popular. Thor is Odin's son, one of the most significant deities in Norse mythology. He was the god of thunder, lightning, and fertility. Thor was known for his strength which is why he was the guardian of Asgard. Asgard is the realm where many Norse deities reside. Thor's weapon, Mjollnir, was a huge and powerful hammer. It was dwarves that made Mjollnir for Thor, and he used it against powerful evil creatures like snakes and giants. Thor is often depicted as a bearded man with red hair. Although most people associate Thor with thunder, he also played a huge role in agriculture. People often presented offerings to Thor during times of drought so he would bless them with rain.

Loki

Forget everything you have learned about Loki from the movies because his role in Norse mythology is different and smaller than that of Odin and Thor. Loki was a demi-god and Thor's brother. He was the god of mischief, trickery, and fire. He wasn't a deity that people worshiped or revered, as he didn't provide any help or bestow any blessings. Loki thrived on chaos; his main purpose was to play tricks and cause trouble for deities and mankind. There was no deeper meaning for his actions; everything he did was for his own enjoyment. Like Odin, Loki also had shapeshifting abilities and could transform into a man, a woman, or any type of animal.

Frigga

Frigga, or Frigg, was Odin's wife and was often referred to as the Queen of Heaven. She was the mother to three of Odin's sons: Hermod, Baldur, and Höðr. She was the goddess of marriage and fertility and could see the future. Frigga was very wise and intelligent, even wiser than Odin himself. There is a beautiful meaning behind Frigga's name. It is derived from the Norse word fríja, which translates to "to love." Have you ever wondered why many people prefer to get married on Fridays? This is meant to honor Frigga, who this day was named after her.

Heimdall

Heimdall was Thor's son, and he was the god of light. He had the gift of prophecy and was able to see the future. His senses were sharper than many other gods. He could hear everything around him, even in the far distance. He also could see for hundreds of miles, whether day or night. He is often depicted with a gold tooth. He guarded the Bifrost Bridge, the bridge (path) between Asgard and Earth. Heimdall plays a very prominent role in Norse mythology as he guarded all the gods in Asgard, and he is the one that will warn them when Ragnarok (the end of the world) occurs. He is believed to blow on a magical horn that would alert all of Asgard that the end of the world is here.

Zeus

Shifting from Norse deities to Greek ones. Since he was the king of all gods, Zeus was the most significant god in Greek mythology. Zeus killed his father, Kronos, and became the supreme deity and lived on Mount Olympus. He married his sister Hera, the goddess of marriage. Zeus was a very powerful god responsible for everything in the universe, like time, fate, order, and the weather. As a result, he was highly revered among the ancient Greeks.

Poseidon

Poseidon was the Greek god of the seas, horses, storms, and earthquakes. He is often depicted holding a trident with a dolphin by his side. Like the seas he ruled over, Poseidon's temper was unpredictable. He could experience moments of peace and tranquility; at other times, he could be violent and angry like a storm.

Minerva

Minerva was the Roman goddess of arts and wisdom, similar to her Greek counterpart Athena. She was the daughter of Jupiter, the chief deity in ancient Rome. However, Jupiter swallowed Minerva's mother, Metis, when she was pregnant with her because there was a prophecy that this child would be stronger than he ever was. When inside Jupiter, Metis created armor and made weapons for her daughter, which Minerva used to make so much noise. Jupiter couldn't handle the noise, so he split his own head open, and Minerva was born from it.

The Significance of Nature in Ancient Paganism

Nature was highly revered in ancient Paganism. The ancient pagans believed they could recognize the divine in nature. They regarded nature as something sacred. Birth, life, and death were more than just cycles that every person must experience; they carried deep spiritual meaning. Mankind didn't hold any significance over other creatures or natural objects. They were equal to animals, plants, trees, etc. However, it is essential to note that pagans didn't worship nature but only held it in high regard because they believed that the divine was everywhere.

Ancient Pagan Festivals

Every belief has its own festivities where its followers either celebrate a deity or a change in the seasons, and Paganism is no different. Here, we will cover some of the most popular ancient pagan festivals, many of which pagans celebrate to this day.

Samhain

Samhain took place on the Celtic new year, which was October 31. Halloween is also a popular festival that takes place on this date. In fact, modern-day Halloween was heavily influenced by the celebrations of Samhain. The word "Samhain" means summer's end, and it celebrates the end of the harvest season and the beginning of the dark and cold weather. Samhain was a very special time for the Celts as it allowed them to connect with their ancestors. They believed an invisible veil separated the physical world from the other world. This veil was at its weakest during Samhain, which allowed the spirits of the dead to travel between worlds. Besides the spirits of the dead, ghosts, fairies, and demons were all free to visit this realm.

Saturnalia

Saturnalia was an ancient Roman festival that celebrated the winter solstice. As the name indicates, this festival celebrated the Roman god of agriculture, Saturn. Similar to Halloween, Christmas was also heavily influenced by Saturnalia. The festival occurred in early December and often lasted for a week. During this festival, the ancient Romans lived a life of extreme pleasure and did everything in excess. Just like Christmas traditions, people ate, drank, and exchanged gifts.

Yule

Yule was a Celtic festival that took place in mid-winter. This is the time of year when the days would begin to be longer, and this festival celebrates the return of the sun. People celebrated this festival by drinking, exchanging stories, and lighting bonfires. They also burned Yule logs for twelve days so its light could vanquish evil spirits that appear on the dark days of winter. Christmas has also borrowed many of its traditions from this festival.

Imbolc

Imbolc was a Celtic festival that took place on February 1st and second. This festival occurs after the winter solstice and before the spring equinox in various places around Europe. Pagans revered and celebrated the goddess of arts and crafts, Brigid, on this day.

Akitu

Akitu was a Babylonian festival that celebrated the beginning of spring. The festival revolved around the story of the marriage between the Babylonian chief god Marduk and the goddess of the Earth, Ishtar. According to the story, Marduk traveled to marry his bride Ishtar at night. During Akitu, the ancient Babylonians celebrated the union between heaven and the earth, just like the one between Marduk and Ishtar.

Wepet Renpet

Wepet Renpet was an ancient Egyptian festival, and it was celebrated on the ancient Egyptian new year, which took place on September 11th on the Gregorian calendar. However, the date of this festival wasn't fixed as it mainly depended on the flow of Egypt's most significant river, the Nile. The festival also celebrated the death and resurrection of Osiris, the god of agriculture, fertility, resurrection, and the afterlife. Osiris was murdered by his brother Seth, but his devoted wife Isis found him and brought him back to life, where he then became the god of the dead and the underworld. Wepet Renpet was one of the most popular festivals in ancient Egypt since Osiris had many followers at the time.

As you may have noticed, almost all pagan festivals involve the beginning, end, or a prominent time in each season. Most pagans' festivals usually mark a specific time during the seasons, which shows how significant of a role the four seasons played in their celebrations.

Paganism focused on the worship of many deities and allowed people to worship as many gods as they wanted. Their deities played a significant role in their lives as the people assigned a god to every aspect of their lives to protect them and provide help when all earthly methods failed. Nature, gods, and festivals all played a huge role in Paganism and helped influence many neo-pagan beliefs.

Chapter 3: Neopaganism vs. Wicca

As is the natural course of traditions, Paganism as a religion has evolved. The way it's practiced in modern times is often very different from the ancient customs. Due to the diversity of the followers' needs, more branches became available, and many other religions have left their mark on Pagan practices. These belief systems are classified under an umbrella term called Neopaganism. One of the most widely recognized branches of Neopaganism is Wicca, which is one of the newest forms of Pagan spiritual practices. Seeing how both draw inspiration from ancient pagan traditions, including the festivities, rituals, and more, *Neopaganism* and *Wicca* are often mistakenly used interchangeably. The similar cultural references in modern media and pop culture don't help dispel the confusion. However, as you'll see from this chapter, the two are entirely separate religions. Not only are their definitions different, but they often have different approaches to their practices.

One of the most widely recognized branches of Neopaganism is Wicca.
https://www.pexels.com/photo/man-people-woman-art-7190312/

Are Neopagans and Wiccans the Same?

One of the reasons Neopaganism and Wicca are often depicted as one and the same is that almost all Wicca practitioners are Neopagans - at least to a certain degree. However, not all Neopagans are Wiccans because many choose to follow different paths that have nothing to do with what modern Wicca stands for. To make things more confusing, not all Wiccans practice their craft similarly. Some will openly embrace witchcraft - while others choose to leave magic out of their practices. Others practice magic without embarking on a pagan path. Instead, they remain faithful to religions that marked their past because they feel they align with their values more. Whichever course one takes is a highly personal choice each practitioner can make on their own accord. The beauty of spirituality-based religions is that when following them, you're free to act in whichever way feels right to you. If you have trouble understanding the difference between the two approaches, the rest of this chapter will help clarify things. It can be a great stepping stone if you decide to embrace the Wiccan path - with or without magic.

What Is Neopaganism?

Neopaganism is defined as a collective term for several types of spirituality - which are more or less based on ancient pagan traditions. Some of the most popular Pagan belief systems practiced today are Asatru, Thelema, Druidism, Heathenry, Shamanism, Animism, and Reconstructionism. There are also Pagans who don't follow any specific religion. They try to adopt the ancient Celtic Pagan traditions of relying on nature for sustenance, guidance, and spiritual growth.

Originating from centuries-old Paganism, Neopaganism has emerged as a way to bring forward religions based on pre-Christian beliefs throughout Europe. It started as a byproduct of the counterculture spreading through North America during the 1960s. At that time, it was primarily based on environmentally conscious beliefs and equality expressed in new, creative ways. While inspired by the ancient Pagan traditions, it was presented to people in a way they needed it. This trend has continued in our now technologically advanced world, where there is even more need for finding a connection with nature. Since Neopaganism is not a centralized religion, the number of ways one can express Neopagan beliefs is nearly limitless. Most practitioners work alone throughout the year and gather during festivities during the equinoxes and other sabbats. Despite meeting only a handful of times a year, most Neopagans are incredibly supportive of each other's practices and have similar values.

Life-affirming is one of the qualities all Neopagans hold in high regard, regardless of their branch and any other beliefs they might have. They acknowledge that life has a beginning, a middle, and an end. Death, like in nature, is just a part of human life. It often comes with pain in suffering, but that's just the way things go in the natural world. For that reason, instead of fearing the dark days that come before death, many Neopagans seek wisdom and peace in the late stages of their lives. They also revere this stage because, for them, the purpose of life is found in the present existence and not after it. They live in the moment because they know they can learn from each experience. Difficulties are viewed as opportunities and not as punishment.

Similarly to their ancestors, the Pagans of today are typically either polytheistic or eventually duotheistic, meaning the followers worship several or at least two deities. Neopagans may even worship modern gods or choose to make new interpretations of the ancient ones. The archetypes of the Horned God, the Triple Moon Goddess, or the Dying God are still present. However, some practitioners will refer to the divine feminine as the Great Goddess of the Earth, Gaia. Male deities may also be called different names that complement their female counterparts.

For Neopagans, the divine power often transcends gender - which is yet another powerful reason for the resurgence of this religion. Some deities have both male and female elements - and even those with only one aspect are held in high esteem, regardless of gender. This allows practitioners to honor their male and female deities through the same traditions and practices. It also enables women to practice their religion the same way men do. For Neopagans, the image of the Goddess represents change - and her power is evidenced in nature. The cyclical shifts of feminine power that creates life, nurture it, and die afterward are also honored in this religion. This reverence is reflected in the movement of the celestial bodies, the seasons, and the life cycle of living beings. Pantheism is also a common belief among Neopagans. They believe that people have divine qualities - and when they reach for divine wisdom, they have to look inside and not outside themselves. Instead of looking for higher power, they practice delving deeper into their subconscious. Because, once again, power comes from nature, and it's inside everyone - and everyone can access it if they look deep enough into themselves. Others see gods as literal beings with specific needs and preferences.

Whether performed on special occasions or daily, the work of a Neopagan is always intentional. For example, celebrating the solar solstices and turning of the seasons is always done at the right time on what they call the "Wheel of the Year." In addition, they often create new rituals or tailor the old ones if they feel this helps them get better results. This often helps them enhance their experiences and allows them to connect with nature even more.

Another common element that defines Neopagans is the reverence of nature or the earth itself. Nature is sacred and everywhere, permeating everything with its essence - from humans to every other living being. This intrinsic value drives Neopagans to stay immersed in their environment, communicate with it, honor it, and stay true to it. Whether the practitioners work alone or belong to a community with whom they share their cultural beliefs, they'll try to remain as true to nature as possible. In today's world, people are often disconnected from nature, and one of the goals of contemporary pagans is to change that. They feel that the only way to save and honor the natural world is to express its sacredness and renew their connection with it. They often use the term "re-enchanting nature," which means nothing more than slowing down and allowing one to see just how precious the natural world is.

Neopaganism encompasses an incredibly eclectic and colorful set of practices. It embraces the teachings of ancient wisdom, the expression of new ideas, and everything in between. Just as there is diversity in nature, so are the different cultures and ideological beliefs. Neopagans honor this diversity and don't accept any form of intolerance and discrimination towards other ideas. No matter how firmly a practitioner stands in their beliefs, they'll always listen to what others say without prejudice or judgment. It may not work for them, but they see no reason why it couldn't work for others. According to Neopagans, everyone is free to decide what they believe in, and there is no absolute truth.

Apart from nature and life, Neopagans also hold their own bodies to be sacred. They use their body to communicate with the natural world, which means they rely on it on a regular basis. Because of this, they always strive to nourish and listen to its cues when something is wrong or needs to be changed in order to avoid an injury or illness. They allow themselves to enjoy everything that feels good for their bodies, from food to exercise to meditation - without guilt or the need to explain this to others.

What Is Wicca?

While Wicca is also an Earth-based religion, it has a slightly different approach to spiritual development. It relies primarily on magic to achieve this and many other specific goals. It was founded by Gerard Gardner in the late 1930s. After traveling through Asia and being fascinated by the different religions he encountered on his journey, Gardner arrived in England. There, he was introduced to a coven of Pagan practitioners who delved into witchcraft. Instead of embracing this practice as it is, Gardner formed a new one. He then incorporated elements from several other religions he was familiar with. This new religion was called Wicca, which means "witch" in Old English. Soon after it was founded, Wicca began to spread from England to Ireland, Scotland, and Wales. A couple of decades later, in the 1970s, it reached other continents, including North America. However, it took another decade until people started to view Wicca as a legitimate religion and not just a few people interested in the occult and Satanism.

Unlike traditional Neopagan beliefs, followers of Wicca rarely worship more than two deities. Because of this, the God and Goddess are often viewed as the only two deities you can ask for guidance. The male deity is also identified as Cerrunos, the Lord of Death, the Horned God, or the Leader of the Wild Hunt. Wiccan traditions with a closer connection to nature may also call him the Oak King or the Holly King - and honor him as such in festivals and ceremonies. The foremost Pagan female deity is the Triple Goddess. She has all three faces of a woman - the Maiden, the Mother, and the Crone. She may also bear the name of Aradia. Gardener's Wicca was only centered around one deity who could take on both male and female attributes. Although, according to Gardner, it didn't really matter whether it was male or female as long as people respected both when they worshipped.

Because Wicca is still loosely based on ancient Pagan traditions, it's not surprising that the deities they honor were all members of the Celtic pantheon. Of course, there are always exceptions to the rule. For example, some practitioners remain faithful to the gods from the religion they previously followed, despite embracing Paganism. There are also atheistic branches of contemporary Paganism - whose followers don't honor any deities.

Some Wiccans worship only one god or goddess. Whereas others honor several of them, calling on them for specific purposes. For example, there is a branch that emphasizes the role of feminine energies. Their followers only worship the Goddess and don't recognize male energy - deviating from the ancient Celtic Pagan customs. Honoring one deity is also common for those who converted from monotheistic religions like Christianity, which only acknowledges one god. Wiccans who convert from these religions often keep worshiping the same entity they worshiped before. They do it with the addition of higher spiritual goals and possibly magic.

Since Wicca is even named after the practitioners of witchcraft, it has become universally accepted that all Wiccans practice this art. However, this isn't always the case. Wiccans highly emphasize spiritual growth because it promotes the development of one's intuition. Wiccans use magic by connecting their energy to the energy contained in magical tools, elements of nature, and even inanimate objects. To do this, they must learn to rely on their intuition. They believe that the knowledge of how to harness magic is held in the subconscious - and the shortest way to access it is by listening to one's gut feelings. Once they gain access to magical energies, they'll know how to manipulate them to manifest the changes they want to make.

Wicca can be practiced in groups (or covens, as witches call them) or alone. One enters a coven after a brief induction period and remains as long as one chooses. Whether you wish to practice alone or in a coven, you can incorporate several different ideas into your practice. Some of the common branches of modern Wicca are Celtic, Eclectic, Faerie, Gardnerian (or original as it is the one based on Gardner's ideas), and Ceremonial Magic. All these originate from Paganism, but their founders have made sure to point out the distinction between their ideas and the traditional Pagan approach to life.

Witchcraft in Wicca can be used as a simple tool to harness magical energy without the practitioners adopting any spiritual beliefs. To practice witchcraft, you don't have to follow Pagan traditions like the reverence of nature, deities, or the life cycle. So, as you see, the connection between Neopaganism, Wicca, and witchcraft is much more complicated than how it's represented in mainstream media. Whichever path you choose is based on your personal preferences. However, there is a chance that you won't be able to avoid at least two of these three terms interfering with each other.

In Wicca, practitioners can choose how to interact with the deities, spiritual guides, and other entities they may rely on for guidance, healing, or magical help for various purposes. Some will freely interact with the deities, and they consider them quite approachable. Other Wiccans view the deities only as personifications of values and attributes they want to gain. They will aim to harness their wisdom through specific tools and not by communicating with a particular deity they need help from.

Another common element of all Wiccan approaches is the Wiccan Rede. This dictates that anything is permitted as long as it doesn't harm anyone. This is particularly significant because many Wiccans can distinguish between dark and light magic. Most will only work with light magic as they want to ensure that the way they manipulate energy won't harm anyone. Many advise that the first person to experience the negative effects is typically the practitioner themselves - forcing them to abide by the law of threefold return. According to Wicca, all of the practitioner's actions (good or bad) come back three times. Consequently, the triple effects would affect them the most, whether the act was aimed at them or someone else.

Wiccans show reverence for the four primordial elements of nature (air, fire, water, and earth). Traditionally, they tie these to a fifth element (the spirit). In their magical practices, Wiccans often associate the elements with the four states of matter (plasma, solid, gas, and liquid). Knowing which element controls which state allows them to infuse their tools with magical energy.

Besides the elements of nature, Wiccans also honor the seasons, similarly to how the Pagan ancestors did. According to them, each season represents the end of a significant period in people's lives and nature - and the beginning of another one. The veneration of the Horned God and the Triple Goddess of fertility also stems from these traditions. In addition, following the Western esotericism from which Wicca draws some of its ideas and basics, the religion promotes the need for spiritual development through its connection with nature and its magic. Even if not all practitioners rely on magic directly, they can still use it to spread good energy, peace, and love.

Are You a Neopagan, Wiccan, or Both?

If you're still unsure whether Wicca or any other form of Paganism is the right path for you to follow, the following quiz will help you decide:

- Do you find grounding exercises enough to reconnect with nature?

- Do you feel the need to honor several deities and revere the change they bring to people's lives?

- Do you embrace life's cycle as a whole, even its dark side, knowing that it only leads to rebirth?

- Do you prefer general life-affirming practices over the ones that lead to specific goals with the help of specific tools?

- Do you identify yourself with the beliefs of Asatru, Heathenry, Druidism, or any other Pagan practice that doesn't rely on witchcraft?

- Do you prefer ancient techniques over modern approaches in Pagan practices?

If you answered most of these questions with yes, you are a Neopagan. You prefer following nature's rhythm and letting it guide you instead of relying on magical acts. If you answered most of the questions with no, you are a Wiccan. Magic is part of your life, and you feel it's helping you achieve your spiritual goals or anything else you desire. You are both if you have an almost equal number of yes and no answers. You are a Neopagan who embraces ancient traditions and combines them with the regular use of magic in their practices. You may not use magic daily, but you'll definitely reach for it if you really need to.

Chapter 4: Practical Wicca

Now that you've learned the background of Wicca, it's time for you to explore the practical side of it. In this chapter, you'll find hands-on advice on how to start your practice with the essentials like setting an altar, making a book of shadows, casting a protective circle, and more. Feel free to use the tools, methods, and spells you've given here, or create some of your own traditions with items you feel more aligned with.

Most Wiccan traditions recommend using a symbol for the god and the goddess.
https://www.pexels.com/photo/two-women-with-rings-in-black-jackets-touching-bull-skull-7189116/

Preparing for Work

Since Wiccan magic is so personal, you'll need to prepare yourself before any work (including the basics like setting up an altar). First, you'll need to cleanse your body and mind. You can do this by taking a cleansing bath, meditation, or even simple breathing exercises. Smudging is another excellent option for cleaning. You can use it to dispel negative energy from your sacred space and purify your body and senses. Apart from these preparation methods, you should always wash your hands before you do anything relating to magic. It's also a good idea to swipe the floors and air the room before you get to work.

Timing is crucial for magical practices. You can optimize your timing by choosing the right time of the day, week, or month when you start gathering supplies, decorating, and forming your intentions and spells. For example, you should think about setting an altar at sunset or after it under the moonlight - even if you're doing a simple one for daily practice. Decorations and certain tools should only be used at specific times, and using them at any other time may render them ineffective. It's also crucial to get your intention sorted out in time. Without a clear intent, you won't be able to focus your energy and reveal any wisdom you require for success. Ideally, you should coordinate forming your intention with the time you begin preparing the tools you use for every spell, ritual, and other magical act.

Creating an Altar

While having an altar isn't a prerequisite for successful magical work, it does help focus your energy and thoughts in the right direction. With a Wiccan practice, you'll need to hone your intuition, and the best way to do this is to have space dedicated to your spiritual and magical work. As a novice, you won't have to create an elaborate space - a simple altar will be more than enough to help you practice. Here is how to create a simple Wiccan altar.

Gathering Basic Supplies

First, you'll need a flat surface to work on. This can be anything from a simple tabletop to the top of your nightstand. Ensure you only keep items related to your intention or practice on it.

Depending on your preferences, you can get a cloth to cover the altar as a means to define it as your sacred space. You'll need supplies to represent the four elements, the four directions, and the deity, spirit, or guide you're working with. Most Wiccan traditions recommend using a symbol for the god and the goddess. This can be as simple as using a bowl as a symbol of the divine feminine and a knife to represent masculine energy. Don't forget the pentagram, either. As an ultimate pagan symbol, the pentagram represents all four elements united in the first one - the spirit. Other supplies you need will be related to the specific work you plan to do and the season. Offerings and decorations like flowers, leaves, fruit, and veggies should all be seasonal.

Choosing the Location

Where you set up an altar depends on your preferences but also on your intention. Different purposes may require you to set up the altar in different directions. Here are some ideas on how to place your altar:

- **Facing East** - Is the most common choice as it corresponds to several intentions.

- **Facing South** - It works best for inspiration, courage, or making significant decisions.

- **Facing West** - This is the direction that symbolizes emotions and enhances them.

- **Facing North** - Associated with abundance and prosperity, the north is best when seeking growth.

Use a compass to identify the directions or follow the sun's movements. However, if you're working with limited space and have only one option, don't worry. You can always set up the altar where you can keep it long-term and enhance your intention in other ways.

Setting Up the Altar

Now it's time you place everything you gathered on your altar. Here is how to do it:

- Take a deep breath and release it slowly. Place the symbol of God and the Goddess in the center of the altar.

- Facing east, place the representation of the air element. In Wicca, this is typically done with feathers. These also represent the powers of the mind - both imaginative and rational. You're combining these two powers during your spiritual practice.

- Moving towards the south, you'll place the symbol of fire, like an orange candle (unlit) or a picture of a fire. It's associated with will, energy, power, and powerful animals. This applies only to the Northern hemisphere. In the Southern hemisphere, fire is linked to the north.

- West can be represented by shells and other remnants of the creatures living in the water. It's linked to love and other fluid emotions.

- North is linked to the earth and is best represented by a cup of soil, salt, grains, or seeds. If you use the latter, you can take the seeds with you after your work is done and plant them somewhere where they can grow and thrive - or toss them out to feed the birds. Earth is also linked to life, so these are great ways to help nature create and nourish living beings.

- Spread any seasonal or intentional decorations (including the offerings) around the tools already on the altar.

- Place the pentagram in front of all the other tools and decorations.

- Take a deep breath and give thanks for what you were able to create. No matter how simple your altar is, the symbols you place on them will be as powerful as you make them.

- Invite the deities and spirits you want to work with and express gratitude for their help.

Making a Book of Shadows

The book of shadows is a collection of wisdom you gather over time. You'll need a blank notebook or maybe a binder. The latter is great for rearranging the contents later on. Whatever you choose, make sure it's good quality. After all, the book of shadows is a magical tool you'll use a lot - and it needs to last. Here are some ideas on what to include in your book:

- **Rules:** Even if you practice alone, you'll probably have boundaries and values you'll want to stick to. Write down what you think is acceptable to you and what's not.

- **Deities:** Whether you honor one deity, two, or more, it's a good idea to have a page dedicated to each of them. You can write any legends and correspondents associated with them, their preferred offerings, etc.

- **Dedication:** Recording the date you've become committed to a cause is a great way to honor it. You can dedicate yourself to a deity, spirit, healing, or other causes.

- **Correspondences:** Apart from the deities, you'll also need to learn the correspondences for the moon phases, energies, herbal ingredients, and much more. Enlisting them in your book of shadows will help you keep everything in one place so you can look up anything you need.

- **Significant Rituals and Ceremonies:** Record all the eight sabbats of the Wheel of the Year and the directions for any other rites and ceremonies you want to work on.

- **Recipes:** Your book of the shadow is also the perfect place to catalog all your recipes for healing concoctions, ointments, offerings, your unique recipes for holiday feasts, herbal blends, and much more.

- **Spells:** You can record the existing spells you prefer to work on or craft new ones - although many witches have a specific spellbook or grimoire for that purpose.

- **Divination:** If you practice divination, you can use your book of shadows to list all the information you need for your art. You can also record your sessions' results and revisit them to see how successful they were.

Casting a Circle

Wiccans use circles for protection, cleansing, and defining a place as sacred and safe for spells, rituals, and spiritual communication. A circle may also help you focus your energy - and the way you cast it will make everything even more personal. To form a sacred circle, you'll rely on the four directions and their associations with the four natural elements - just as you do when setting up an altar.

You'll Need the following:

- Salt - for the earth element
- Incense - for the fire element
- Feather - for the air element
- Water - for the water element
- A cloth to sit on (if you're working outside)
- A compass
- A space that's about 9ft in diameter
- A 4.5ft long cord
- A bundle of dried sage
- A crystal or a wand for directing the energy
- A symbol for the God and the Goddess

Instructions:

1. Gather all your supplies and find north on your compass. Lay out the cloth if you're outside.

2. Facing north, place the symbol of the male deity on your left side and the female one on your right side.

3. Take a few grounding breaths and visualize a green light enveloping your feet. Picture it traveling upwards toward your body.

4. Now visualize a white light enveloping your head and traveling down, meeting and mixing with the green one. When they do, they'll ground you and chase away the negative energy from and around you.

5. Visualize the lights departing and stretch your body to release any residual tension.

6. Take the string, and hold it over the salt while you place the latter on the north.

7. Turn the string slightly to the right to face east. Place the feather on the ground. You can secure it with a rock if you're outside.

8. Turn to face south and repeat with the incense, then finally with the water when facing West.

9. Facing one direction at a time, recite:

    "North, I welcome you, and I ask for your protection.

    East, I welcome you, and I ask for your wisdom.

    South, I welcome you, and I ask for your warmth.

    West, I welcome you, and I ask for your cleansing power."

10. Light the sage and start smudging your circle, starting North.

11. Walk in a clockwise direction 3 times while saying:

12. "With the power *of three, I banish negativity."*

You can now cast the spell or perform the ritual of your choice. When you're done, don't forget to close the circle. The simplest way to do this is to face each direction and express your gratitude for their assistance in your work.

Simple Wiccan Spells and Rituals

Your best work will always be the one that's done with spells and rituals coming from your intention and tailored to fit it the best. However, if you're unsure where to begin, here are a few spells and rituals to help you get started on your Wiccan journey.

Freezing Spell against Bad Intentions

Whether it's people who spread rumors about you or someone who wants to harm you, these spells will help you against them. It's a harmless spell designed to keep toxic individuals away from you.

You'll Need the following:

- Water
- A zip-lock bag
- A piece of paper
- A pen or any other writing instrument

Instructions:

1. Fill up the bag with water. Leave about ⅓ at the top of the bag empty, so you can close it.

2. Write your intention on the paper. Be specific but leave room for a spell to work. For example, even if you want to keep a specific person out, don't use just their name. Write that you want the person to be bidden to stay away from you instead.

3. Fold the paper (so it fits the bag), and recite the following while focusing your energy on your intention:

   "I will now freeze this person out of my life to prevent them from hurting me."

4. Put the folded paper in the zip-lock bag with the water, and place it in the freezer.

5. Wait until the spell begins to work. Be patient, as this may take time, especially if you don't have too much experience yet.

6. When you feel the spell working, thaw the ice and bury the paper in the soil.

7. Pour the melted water over it and give thanks.

A Ritual for Success

This simple spell will help you manifest your wishes for success more efficiently. It works best for smaller goals, so remember to focus on the present when casting it.

You'll Need the following:

- Up to 20 drops of liquid camphor
- 1-2 large bay leaves
- A marker

Instructions:

1. Write your name and date of birth on one side of the bay leaves.

2. Write your intention on the other side of the leaves. Use short, present tense sentences, like:
   "I have a job."

3. While writing your intentions, focus on believing they've already come true.

4. Move the bay leaves in the air three times. This will communicate your wishes to the element.

5. Put the leaves in camphor, and let the letters dissolve slowly.

6. Take a final deep breath, and while you exhale, express gratitude to the air for granting you your wish.

Talisman with Protective Herbs

With this powerful talisman, you can protect yourself and your home from malicious influences. Activate it before significant magical work and when you think someone's trying to harm you with dark magic.

You'll Need the following:

- 1 Glass container with a lid
- 1 teaspoon of dried dill
- 1 teaspoon of dried and crushed bay leaves
- 1 teaspoon of dried sage
- 1 teaspoon of crushed black peppercorns
- 1 teaspoon of anise
- 1 teaspoon of garlic powder
- ½ cup of salt
- 1 teaspoon of fennel
- 1 teaspoon of dried basil
- 1 teaspoon of cloves

Instructions:

1. Place every ingredient in the jar, close it and shake it nine times to mix everything until well combined.

2. Then, recite the following spell:

   "Healing herbs and purifying salts of nine

   Help me guard this space of mine."

3. Place the jar on your altar if you only need protection for yourself and your sacred place during magical work.

4. If you need protection for your entire home, try setting the jar in the middle of your house. Make sure you keep it

where it won't be disturbed. Moving it after setting it can reduce its effects.

5. Replace it every few months to ensure you remain protected from negative influences.

Disclaimers

Wiccan magic is highly personal. You rely on your own ability to manifest your desires. For this reason, you should only practice magic if you can keep your psychological and spiritual well-being in check. If your mental abilities are less than optimal for performing mundane tasks, you should not use them for magic, either. There are plenty of ways to boost your mental health, including meditation you can do at your altar. You can take advantage of the healing energy of the sacred space without focusing on the magic. Do a quick check of your mental state Before you start preparing for magical work and see if there are any stressors you have to deal with before you can proceed.

Wiccan traditions encourage using magic only for good and reject any negative purposes. Make sure that everything you do is for positive purposes and that you're allowed to do whatever you plan. Consult the deity or spiritual guide you plan to work with and ask them if it's a good idea.

Chapter 5: Norse Paganism and Asatru

Norse paganism is a set of beliefs and practices based on worshiping ancient Scandinavian gods. It is also known as Asatru, which means "faith in the gods." Norse paganism was the religion of the Viking people, who lived in what is now Scandinavia, Iceland, and Greenland. Today, many people practice Norse paganism, drawn to its rich mythology and practical worldview. Followers of the tradition believe in balancing these forces within themselves. They also believe that humans are an important part of the natural world and should live in harmony with nature.

Today, many people practice Norse paganism, drawn to its rich mythology and practical worldview.
https://www.pexels.com/photo/food-wood-nature-sun-6806402/

Norse paganism has a strong emphasis on personal growth and experimentation. Its practitioners believe that everyone has the potential to learn and grow, regardless of their background or station in life. As such, Norse pagans often seek out new experiences and perspectives. They value trials and challenges as opportunities to learn and grow. This open-minded approach to life can be refreshing for those who feel bogged down by the grind of everyday life.

In addition to its practical benefits, Norse paganism offers a deep connection to the natural world and our ancestors. For many people, this is a key reason for practicing this ancient faith. When we connect with nature, we remember that we are part of something larger than ourselves. We also remember our ancestors who came before us and the traditions they passed down. This can give us a sense of rootedness and belonging that is hard to find in today's fast-paced world.

This chapter will explore this fascinating religion's origins, history, and symbols. We will also examine the belief system and discuss some important concepts central to Norse paganism. Finally, we will look at some of the myths and legends associated with this faith.

Origins and History

The Norse pagan religion, also known as Asatru, is a polytheistic religion that stems from the practices of the ancient Germanic people. This ancient belief system is based on the pre-Christian mythology of northern Europe. Norse pagans believe in an afterlife and that the soul is reborn into another body after death. They also believe in reincarnation and that the world will one day be destroyed and rebuilt. Many modern pagans practice Asatru as a form of spirituality rather than religion. For them, it is a way to connect with their ancestors and nature. It is also a way to live in harmony with others and the world around them. Asatru is not just a set of beliefs but a way of life.

The ancient Norse people were polytheistic, meaning they worshiped multiple gods and goddesses. The most important deities in the Norse pantheon were Odin, Thor, and Freyja. These gods were associated with war, fertility, and wisdom, respectively. The

Norse pantheon also included several other gods and goddesses, each of whom had their own areas of expertise. The Norse religion was based on a cosmology that revolved around the concept of nine worlds. Midgard, the world of humans, was considered the center of the universe by worshippers. There were four worlds surrounding Midgard: those of the giants, elves, dwarves, and the gods and goddesses. And in between these worlds, there was a mighty tree called Yggdrasil that linked them together. Norse Pagans believe in an afterlife and that those who die bravely in battle will spend eternity in Valhalla. They also believe in reincarnation and that souls can be reborn into different forms. Modern practitioners of Norse Paganism often hold rituals and celebrations outdoors, and many still live close to nature. For them, religion is not just a set of beliefs but a way of life.

Symbols and Cosmology

Norse paganism is a complex and fascinating belief system. It has a rich history and a truly unique cosmology. The most prominent symbol in Norse paganism is the hammer of Thor, which is a powerful symbol of protection. Other notable symbols include the Viking ship, which represents travel and exploration, and the Yggdrasil, which symbolizes the interconnectedness of all things. Valhalla is an integral part of Norse paganism as it is seen as a place where brave warriors can go after they die. It symbolizes the value of bravery and courage in Norse culture. Additionally, Valhalla provides comfort to those who lost loved ones in battle. They know that they are in a place where they can feast and fight forever.

Afterlife and Ancestor Worship in Norse Paganism

In Norse paganism, the concept of the afterlife and ancestor worship is deeply intertwined. For pagans, the afterlife is not a far-off, ethereal place where we go after death. Instead, it's a realm that exists alongside our own, separated only by a thin veil. Our ancestors live in this realm and can influence our lives—for good or bad. Ancestor worship is, therefore, a very important part of Norse paganism. It's believed that our ancestors can help us in times of need and that they have the power to intercede on our behalf with the gods. To honor our ancestors, modern practitioners often set up shrines in their homes where they keep pictures or other symbolic items that act as reminders. They also make offerings to them—food, drink, or other gifts—at these shrines. These offerings help nourish our ancestors' spirits and keep them happy, bringing blessings into our own lives. Ancestor worship is an important part of Norse paganism as it helps to connect the living with the dead. It is believed that ancestors can help guide and protect their descendants. Additionally, ancestor worship keeps the memory of loved ones alive. It is a way for people to connect with their past and remember those who have come before.

Belief System

The Norse people believed that when they died, their souls would go to either Valhalla (the hall of the slain) or Hel (the realm of the dead). Norse paganism teaches us that death is not the end. It is simply a transition into another stage of life. After we die, our souls go to the underworld, awaiting their final judgment. Suppose we have led good and honorable lives. In that case, we are rewarded with a place in Valhalla—the hall of the gods—where we feast and fight alongside Odin, Thor, and the other gods until the end of time. If we have not, however, our souls are sent to Hel—a dark and dismal realm ruled by the goddess Hela. The souls of murderers and other criminals are said to suffer horribly in Hel. It is, therefore, very important to live good lives so that we may enjoy happy afterlives with our ancestors in Valhalla.

Myths and Lore

The myths and legends associated with Norse paganism are some of the most fascinating stories in all of human history. The sagas and poems of the Norse people tell tales of gods and heroes, dragons and trolls. These stories are a window into the beliefs and values of the ancient Norse people and are often depicted in stories and artwork, which has led to several myths and lore linked to them.

Nordic mythology is full of fascinating and intriguing stories. Many of these stories involve powerful beings and heroic feats and are often steeped in mystery and magic. Some of the most well-known tales from Nordic mythology include the story of Ragnarok (the end of the world) and the story of Odin and his eight-legged horse, Sleipnir. These mythical beings often play an important role in the stories, and many of them have become iconic symbols of Nordic culture.

While some of the stories from Nordic mythology are dark and foreboding, others are lighthearted and fun. Many of the tales include elements of comedy, romance, and adventure. Regardless of their tone, all of the stories from Nordic mythology are fascinating and provide a glimpse into the culture and beliefs of the people who created them.

Heathenry

Heathenry is a polytheistic, indigenous European religion that emphasizes honor, courage, and familial bonds. Modern Heathenry has been influenced by various sources, including Norse mythology, the Icelandic sagas, and other Germanic traditions. Many Heathens see their religion as a way to connect with their ancestors and heritage. Heathenry is a reconstructionist religion, meaning its followers attempt to revive and recreate the beliefs and practices of the ancient Germanic peoples. This often includes studying the old myths and legends and trying to recreate our ancestors' lifestyles. While some people might see this as living in the past, Heathens believe that our ancestors were closer to nature and had a deeper understanding of the world around them.

While Heathenry is not an exclusive religion, most of its followers are of Germanic descent. This includes people from Scandinavia, the British Isles, Germany, Austria, and the Netherlands. In recent years, there has been a growing interest in Heathenry among people of other European backgrounds and those from North America and Australia. There are many different Heathen groups and organizations, each with its own unique take on the religion. Some focus on the worship of specific deities, while others emphasize community and fellowship. Heathens can be involved in various activities, from public rituals to private worship.

If you are interested in learning more about Heathenry, many resources are available online and in bookstores. There are also several active Heathen groups and organizations that can provide support and guidance. Whether you're looking to connect with your ancestry or learn more about ancient religion, Heathenry may be right for you.

Asatru

Even though the term Heathenry is used to refer to the entire religious movement.

Asatru is often preferred as a way to designate different groups within the religion. One of the main groups that followers belong to is Asatru.

The word "Asatru" comes from Old Norse and means "faith in the gods." In its modern form, Asatru is a reconstructionist religion that seeks to revive the polytheistic faith of the ancient Germanic peoples. Although there is no one "Asatru" tradition, common elements are found in many different Asatru practices. These include a focus on the worship of the Aesir (the primary group of Germanic deities) and Vanir (a secondary group of deities), a belief in reincarnation, and the use of runes for divination. Asatru has its roots in the pre-Christian religion of the Germanic peoples. The first written record of Asatru dates back to the late 10th century when it was mentioned in the Icelandic Sagas. Since then, Asatru has undergone several changes and adaptations. In the early 21st century, there were an estimated 5,000-10,000 Asatruar (followers of Asatru) worldwide.

Asatruar believes in the existence of multiple gods and goddesses, each with its own areas of influence. Followers of this religion often celebrate the seasons and major events in the lives of the gods and goddesses. The most important holiday is Yule, which celebrates the sun's rebirth. Other holidays include Ostara (the spring equinox), Midsummer (the summer solstice), and Winternights (a festival honoring the dead).

Modern Asatru Practices

Asatruar typically practices their religion in small groups called "kindreds." These are often organized around a specific god or goddess. Many kindreds also participate in online forums and social media groups. There are several Asatru organizations, each with its own beliefs and practices. The largest Asatru organization is the Asatru Folk Assembly, founded in the United States in 1994. Other notable Asatru organizations include the Odinic Rite (founded in Britain in 1973) and the Ring of Troth (founded in the United States in 1987).

Asatru is an inclusive religion whose followers come from all walks of life. There are no strict rules or guidelines that Asatruar must follow, and people are free to believe and practice as they see fit. This flexibility has likely contributed to Asatru's popularity, as it allows people to tailor their beliefs and practices to their own needs and interests.

Although Asatru is a relatively new religion, it has significantly impacted the world. In recent years, Asatruar has been involved in several high-profile court cases, including one in which an Asatruar was granted the right to wear Thor's hammer pendant as part of his religious beliefs. Asatru is also making an impact beyond the courtroom. In Iceland, for example, an Asatru temple is currently being built, and it is thought to be the first of its kind in the world. This temple will serve as a gathering place for Asatruar and will be used for religious ceremonies and events.

The growth of Asatru is likely to continue in the years ahead as more people become interested in alternative religions. As Asatru becomes more mainstream, we will likely see a greater acceptance of this ancient belief system and its modern adaptations. Its popularity is likely due to several factors, including the rise of the internet and social media, which have made it easier for people to connect with others who share their beliefs. Additionally, the increased interest in paganism and alternative religions has also played a role in Asatru's growth.

Norse Rituals and Rites of Passage

Performing rituals was one way to please the gods and goddesses and to ask for their help or guidance. Different rituals could be performed for different purposes, such as giving thanks or offerings and asking for protection. One popular Norse ritual is called a Blot. This involves making an offering to the gods or goddesses, usually in the form of food or drink. The offering is then shared amongst those taking part in the ritual, and everyone says a prayer or gives thanks. Another popular Norse ritual is called a Sumbel. During this ritual, a horn of a bear or mead is passed around, and everyone drinks and toasts the gods and goddesses. Once again, prayers and thanks may be given during this ritual.

Norse rites of passage are also very meaningful. These can mark major life events such as birth, coming of age, marriage, and death. They often involve special ceremonies and rituals designed to help the person transition into their new phase of life. One of the most significant Norse rites of passage is called a Vala. This involves a woman giving birth in a special hut dedicated to the goddess Freyja. After the baby is born, it is washed in mead and then presented to the gods and goddesses. This ritual ensures that the child will be blessed by the gods and will have a long and prosperous life. Another significant rite of passage is their funeral ritual. In this process, the deceased's body is cremated, and their ashes are scattered at sea. This helps to ensure that their souls find their way to Valhalla, where they will feast and fight alongside the gods for eternity.

Norse rituals can be performed for various purposes, but they all serve to honor the gods and goddesses of Norse mythology. If you are interested in learning more about these rituals, you can take a Norse mythology class or attend a Viking festival.

Norse Magic

The ancient Norse people used runes for writing and divination. Rune is the Old Norse word for "secret" or "mystery." These magical symbols were used to preserve traditions and history and make predictions. Each rune had its own meaning and power, and the wise use of runes was said to be able to bring good fortune or ward off evil. There are different theories about the origins of runes, but most scholars believe that they were developed by the Germanic tribes who lived in northern Europe during the Iron Age. These tribes included the Angles, Saxons, and Jutes, who later migrated to Britain and gave their names to the countries of England, Scotland, and Wales. The runes began as a simplified form of writing, but they acquired magical properties over time. Runes were usually carved into pieces of wood or stone, although they could also be inscribed on metal, bone, or even cloth. The most famous Runes are the Elder Futhark, which consists of 24 symbols. The Elder Futhark was used throughout northern Europe during the Migration period and the early Middle Ages. The Younger Futhark, which has only 16 symbols, was used in Scandinavia during the Viking Age. Runes were also used for divination, and each symbol had its own meaning.

Norse Shamanism - Seidr

The practice of Norse shamanism, Seidr (which will be analyzed further in the following chapters), is an ancient tradition passed down through the generations. It is a form of magic used to connect with the spirits of nature and the cosmos. Seidr is a way of working with the energies of the universe to bring about change in one's life. It is also a way of accessing hidden knowledge and understanding the will of the gods. Seidr is traditionally practiced by those who are known as seers or shamans. These individuals can see into the future and receive guidance from the spirits. Seers can also enter into trances, allowing them to contact the spirits directly. Shamans can use their abilities to help others in their community.

Seidr is a very personal practice, and each shaman has unique ways of working with the spirits. Some use drums or other musical instruments to help them enter into a trance state. Others use chanting or singing to reach the spirit world. The practice of Seidr is not just about entering into trances or contacting spirits. It is also about working with the universe's energies to bring about change. Seers use their abilities to influence the course of events. They can heal the sick, find lost objects, and even bring rain to dry land. Seidr is a powerful tool that can be used for both good and evil.

Seidr is a mystery, and there is much we do not understand about it. However, those practicing it know it is a real and powerful force. Seidr is an important part of Norse culture, and its traditions continue to this day.

The Old Norse religion is an intricate and fascinating belief system that has been around for centuries. It contains interesting stories, myths, and lore that teach us about our ancestors and their beliefs. While there are many aspects of this tradition that we may not be able to understand or agree with today, these beliefs held great importance to the people who practiced them. The Norse religion and its traditions can provide us with a wealth of knowledge about ourselves and life itself. A great deal of meaning is found today in this religion's rituals and mythology, which are important to many people.

Chapter 6: Walking the Seiðr Path

Seidr was the Norse world's most common form of magic and was mainly concerned with issues of fate. Its practitioners could see the traces of fate and subtly change them however they wanted. Their knowledge of divination was used for both good and evil purposes. While they were able to cast curses that hurt people, they also performed protective spells and charms to help others and keep them safe. Those who performed this type of magic typically led nomadic lifestyles, which is why they were not trusted among community members.

The Norse god Odin on his horse Sleipnir.
https://commons.wikimedia.org/wiki/File:Ardre_Odin_Sleipnir.jpg

While women who practiced Seidr were highly respected, men who did it were often scorned. Seidr had an aura of secrecy associated with it, which was a feminine trait in Norse traditions and culture. This is why men who practiced Seidr were thought to be breaking gender norms. This way of thinking also applies to the deities. Even though Odin was believed to be the most skillful practitioner of Seidr in existence, he was mocked for using feminine powers despite his other masculine characteristics.

In this chapter, we'll explore what Seidr is. You'll learn what a Völva is and understand the different levels of trance a shaman can reach. Then, you'll come across a step-by-step guide on how to cast a protective circle, induce a trance state, and practice grounding visualization.

What Is Seidr?

Seidr is a form of Norse shamanism and magic that predates Christianity. It was mainly practiced foretelling fate, identify its path, and manipulate its inner workings to create change. Practitioners could do that by using symbolism to weave desired situations and events into reality. They performed rituals to transport themselves into a trance where they could communicate with the spirit world. Their tasks were mostly done to perform a curse, a blessing, or a prophecy.

Seidr rituals weren't limited to divination and matters of fate. They were also used for clairvoyance, allowing the practitioner to discover the locations of hidden objects and the secrets of the mind. Seidr was also used to heal the sick, attract abundance and good luck, call in fish and animals for food, and control the weather. When used for malicious purposes, Seidr was used to cast curses, such as inducing sickness or making any land barren. Some shamans also told people false futures to lead them toward the wrong, often disastrous, path. Some recipients injured and killed their adversaries in domestic disagreements and during periods of battle due to false readings. Those who mastered the art of weaving to manipulate or change fate were known as the Norns. They were considered to be the most proficient practitioners.

The god Odin and the goddess Freya are two significant Vanir and Aesir deities who mastered the art of Seidr. They were divine archetypes of male and female practitioners. Since this form of magic was very gendered, particularly during the Viking age, it's necessary to keep this distinction in mind.

What Is a Völva?

The goddess Freya modeled the role of the völva. A völva was a woman practitioner of Seidr during the Viking age. Freya is the first deity to bring this type of magic to the realm of the gods. A Völva had an esteemed role in the community as she was considered a healer or spiritual leader in her society. She was usually close to her clan's leaders. Male seidr practitioners were called seers and were rare to find.

A Völva never settled in one area but traveled around different cities. She was offered accommodation in return for magical practices. You can learn more about the Völva from ancient sagas and other transcripts.

Even though they were treated respectfully, Völvas were somewhat segregated from society in negative and positive nuances. A Völva was feared and often stigmatized yet sought-after and esteemed. She is highly comparable to the Veleda, a Germanic prophetess who was very respected among her tribe.

According to Viking culture and traditions, Seidr was considered an inappropriate activity for men. People then were expected to comply with stringent gender roles, which is why it was considered taboo for men to partake in any women-like practices. Therefore, men who practiced Sedr were thought to be "unmanly." This label was a substantial insult to Viking men.

There were numerous reasons for the shunning of male practitioners. Perhaps the most notable is the weaving aspect of the practice, which was among the primary economic contributions of Viking women. That said, some men still engaged in Seidr and even regarded it as their occupation. A few of them had their works recorded in historical sagas.

The leading seer was, of course, the god Odin. Despite his greatness, he was still called unmanly by some. This disapproval, however, often came with nuances of hesitation and uncertainty. Even though practicing this form of magic was perceived as feminine, whoever could do it held immense power. Some male practitioners thought that the perception of society was a small price to pay for the abilities that Seidr offered. Besides, they had none other than Odin, the mighty king of Asgard, to look up to.

Different Levels of Trance

For millennia, humans all across the globe have used numerous techniques to enter trance states, or "altered states of consciousness." Shamans and indigenous groups across nations believed that this state acted as a bridge between the unconscious mind and the world of spirit.

Very few people realize that most major universal belief systems, such as Hinduism and the 3 Abrahamic religions, also have practices that incite subtle trance states. This allows practitioners to connect more effectively with the divine, which essentially grows their faith.

Regardless of your spiritual beliefs, entering a trance state offers numerous benefits, especially if you intend to practice any form of magic.

How Does a Trance State Feel Like?

A trance state is a frame of mind you enter when you're neither sleeping nor entirely conscious. Being in an altered state of consciousness requires you to transport between the conscious and subconscious mind. It's somewhat like zoning out" of reality.

The 5 Levels of Trance State

There are five levels of an altered state of consciousness:

Level 1: Very Light Trance

The first level requires you to increase your self-awareness of your thoughts, feelings, and physical sensations. This state of mind can be accessed via mindful meditation.

Level 2: Light Trance

This frame of mind resembles what it's like to be dreaming. We all experience this altered state of consciousness without realizing it. We all often zone out while driving or reading and just do it

---

automatically.

Level 3: Medium Trance

This trance state entirely shifts your consciousness from your environment. You lose the sense of time and control, or even awareness, of your body.

Level 4: Deep Trance

This is the level of consciousness you'd access if you were hypnotized. The latter is the rapid and somewhat confusing state of consciousness that happens right before you drift off and your conscious mind goes to bed. People who fall into a deep trance usually hallucinate.

Level 5: Very Deep Trance

At this stage, you completely lose consciousness. It is similar to being in a coma or experiencing very deep, dreamless sleep.

Levels 2, 3, and 4 are ideal for spiritual practices.

Step-By-Step Guide

Before we delve into various techniques and exercises, you must know that you should conduct shamanic practices under the supervision of a professional guide. If you wish to practice alone, you must grow your knowledge and expertise in trance and journeying techniques before you move further ahead. It goes without saying that anyone struggling with mental health should not engage in shamanic practices or other rituals.

Casting a Protective Circle

Casting a magic circle can help cleanse and purify your space from undesirable energies. It can help you handle negative people in your life, protect your space from soaking up bad energy, and maintain your peace even if someone is trying to bring you down. People who notice a strange presence or energy in their houses, such as sudden waves of cold air, bizarre noises, and recurrent nightmares, can cast a protective circle to eliminate the unwanted presence.

Magic circles don't only help you get rid of malicious spirits, but they also attract good ones to enter your space. This practice also allows you to direct your own powers toward a sole purpose, which is providing protection and safety from all kinds of harm. You should not attempt any magic ceremony without the presence of a magic circle because otherwise, you wouldn't be able to keep your spell safe from any external, interfering forces. Magic circles help you focus on your intent.

There are numerous ways to cast a magic circle. While some are very simple, others can get extremely complicated. The most popular ways, however, are "Calling in the Four Directions" and "Lesser Banishing Ritual of the Pentagram." The former pertains to indigenous shamanism and is the simpler option. The former comes from Western magical tradition.

Whichever ritual you choose to perform, you need to face each of the four directions so you can pay homage to their power. The shamans embody the directions as animal totems, while in the second method, they are embodied as the Four Archangels. You need to provide an offering of burning tobacco or sage to call in the Four Directions. Some people prefer to raise their hands with their palms facing outward instead.

Face each of the directions as you say the following prayer:

"Guardian of the South, totem of the Serpent, power of the Heart, grant us the gift of your Water medicine so that we may give with our emotions freely and honestly, loving unconditionally.

Guardian of the West, totem of the Jaguar, power of the Body, grant us the gift of your Earth medicine so that we may hold with our bodies, enduring our challenges with strength and grace.

Guardian of the North, totem of the Hummingbird, power of the Mind, grant us the gift of your Air medicine so that we may receive with our minds, always open to wisdom and insight.

Guardian of the East, totem of the Eagle, power of the Spirit, grant us the gift of your Fire medicine, so that we may determine with our spirits, living our lives in harmony with the Great Spirit."

Then, return to your initial position and place your hand over your heart as you recite the rest of the prayer:

"In honor of our ancestors, the star people, the stone people, the plant people, our animal brothers and sisters, sages, healers and teachers past, present and future, and all who dwell herein.

In honor of Mother Earth below, who sustains us. In honor of Father Sky above, who guides us. In honor of the Great Spirit throughout, who has ten thousand names and is the unnamable one.

A-ho!"

Since this is a protection spell, you can tweak the prayer to vocalize your wishes and concerns to your guardians more directly. You can ask them to protect you from the forces that wish to harm you or eliminate any unwanted energies from your life. Suppose you believe you've been subject to a magical attack, which is a very rare occurrence. In that case, you can cast the circle and remain inside it for the entire duration of this attempt. You can absorb sufficient protective power if you sleep inside the circle until sunrise.

Once you've completed your ceremony, you need to close the magic circle by repeating the prayer we mentioned above. However, instead of asking the guardians for their protection or medicine, you should thank them for granting it to you instead. Say your goodbyes before exiting the circle.

Inducing a Trance State

There are a plethora of methods you can try out to induce a trance state. However, the following are among the most popular and easiest techniques to experiment with:

Breathwork:

Changing the rhythm and pace of your breathing is among the most common methods to bring oneself into a trance state. If you're already familiar with some breathing practices, such as pranayama, you can use them to transport yourself into an altered state of consciousness. It doesn't matter which technique you use as long as it's comfortable and doesn't feel forced. You can facilitate the process of entering a trance level of awareness by practicing pranayama or other breathing exercises. This is because these practices allow you to release all mental blocks that hold you back.

Another very popular technique is known as Holotropic breathwork. This practice involves the maintenance of quick and regulated breathing patterns. You must consult your doctor before trying any breathing exercises if you struggle with any health problems.

Recite Mantras and Prayers:

Repeating certain words, making repetitive sounds, or reciting mantras can also be quite helpful. Monks of various religions, including Hinduism, Christianity, and Buddhism, suggest that reciting a mantra can help you alter your consciousness. Prayers mostly only lead to a light state of trance. However, working with prayers that call to you and experimenting with using them in different and unconventional ways can help you transcend the limits of the conscious brain.

Primal Sounds, Beats, and Rhythms:

Have you ever wondered why drums are among the first few elements that come to mind when people think of shamans? Drums are a great way to trigger the trance state that a person needs to embark on their inner journeying practice.

While you can get a bongo, hand drum, or any other drum you like, listening to a primal rhythmic playlist on YouTube will do the trick. Listening to throat singing from indigenous cultures, binaural beats, or repetitive music can be helpful. Avoid listening to songs with words in them unless they're repetitive and are in a language you can't understand. You want to keep your conscious mind as uninvolved as possible.

Grounding Visualization

Step 1: Start by standing with your feet spread apart. Position them firmly on the ground and keep them aligned with your shoulders. Put your arms above your head and extend your fingers toward the ceiling.

Step 2: Visualize bursts of energy leaving the end of your spine and down the soles of your feet. Like tree roots, visualize all this energy digging deep into the ground, penetrating the foundation of your home, the pavement, or the grass. Keep envisioning these roots as they dig through the Earth's soil and crust. Imagine this energy as it travels through the magma and to the planet's core. Feel the energy you can draw from it as it wraps itself around it.

Step 3: Visualize branches growing from your spine, passing through your neck, and reaching out to your head. Visualize branches growing through your arms and through the palms of your hands. Imagine how they would look as they grow higher and into the sky. Envision them as they penetrate the stratosphere reaching through the center of the Universe until they reach the source of creation. Again, imagine the branches as they tap and surround the source, drawing down this energy to you.

Step 4: Imagine yourself as you fill up with all the energy coming from above and below you together. Visualize the divine universal and earthly energies as they combine inside you, making you whole. Visualize this scenario for as long as you need to.

Step 5: Whenever you're ready, visualize the branches as they come back inside. Feel them as they recede into you. Envision the roots receding from the Earth and into your being.

Step 6: Take a couple of deep breaths and bring yourself back to reality.

Now that you have read this chapter, you know everything that you need to know about seidr and its practitioners. You also understand the importance of reaching an altered state of consciousness when practicing inner journeying. Light to deep trance states is ultimately the most effective to work with. Doing breathwork, reciting prayers and mantras, and listening to primal sounds, beats, and rhythms are some of the simplest and most common methods that you can use to induce an altered state of consciousness.

Chapter 7: Runes: History and Theory

Now that you've learned a little more about Norse mythology, you are ready to delve into the use of the runes. These ancient symbols had several purposes throughout history - and this chapter will uncover all of them. You'll see how their use evolved from a complex communication instrument to a simple divination tool, as it is widely known today.

The History of Runes

The early records and the Norse tales indicate that the runes were primarily a communication tool developed by Germanic tribes and used as far back as 50 C.E. However, the earliest known evidence of the runes used as a writing form is documented in a carving that dates back to 400 C.E. According to the lore, the runes were revealed to people by Odin himself. He discovered them during the ordeal he suffered when he was forced to spend nine days and nights hanging from Yggdrasil, also called the "Tree of Life." After the ninth night, he looked down, saw the runes, and was suddenly able to free himself. Although he wielded great power over his followers, Odin realized that the runes held even more wisdom than he possessed and decided to share them with the rest of the deities. He taught them their meaning and use, and, in turn, they passed on this knowledge to people.

People then began to use the runes as letters, organizing them into an alphabet. However, for the ancient Norse, the meaning of each letter wasn't as simple as it is in modern languages. According to them, each rune symbolizes a specific form of energy, a universal thought, or simply an aspect of life. Because of this complex relationship between the runes and their symbolism, the runes were used only by the most educated tribe members. They used the runes to record events and prophecies affecting the tribe or to communicate with other tribes, exchanging information and forging alliances. The primary meaning of the term rune was "mystery" or "message that needs to be kept secret."

The Norse also believed that runes could unlock the future and enable communication across different worlds. According to several Norse myths, runes had magical properties. These allowed people to send and receive messages from higher beings, inducing the deities, ancestral spirits, animals, and even magical inanimate objects.

Each rune was named after what it represented - both in a magical sense and the philosophical one. The runes were initially carved into stone templates, which stood as a testimony to the tribe's hierarchy and achievements. Later, people began to inscribe them on small pieces of stone, bone, metal, or wood and carry them around so they could use them for different purposes. Nowadays, you'll find runes carved or painted on talismans, used as body ink, or written on a piece of paper during magical practices. How runes are written is linked to how their name sounds and which letter they represent in the Norse alphabet. For example, the Tiwaz rune is pictured as an upward-pointed arrow. This depicts the rune as the symbol of the god of war and his habit of traveling across the sky.

Runic alphabets are named "Futharks," after the runes Fehu, Uruz, Thurisaz, Ansuz, Raidho, and Kenaz. These were the first six runes of the oldest known runic alphabet, the Elder Futhark. This alphabet contains 24 runes, which are equivalent to a large number of letters in the Old English language. Most evidence of the use of the Elder Futhark runes has been found on coins, weapons, and garments dating from the Iron Age. In fact, Elder Futhark is still used today, although only for divination and not for writing or communication. The runes in this alphabet were divided into three aetts - each ruled over by a powerful Norse deity. Each aett also represents a specific stage in life - from the earliest success to failure to prospering despite the difficulties.

While the first full alphabet letters were harsh and complex characters, the more recent version, the Younger Futhark, was simpler and contained only 16 runes. This was introduced around 750 CE, with the arrival of the Viking Age. It eventually replaced its predecessor as a writing form throughout Scandinavia. According to historical evidence, at this time, the new runes were used in markets and artifacts depicting the heroic achievements of the tribes. The characters of the Younger Futhark were faster to write, which presumably saved the Vikings time for writing them, so they could be focused on battling instead. Another version, the Anglo-Saxon Futhorc, was developed in England. This one was the expansion of the Elder Futhark - from 24 to 33 characters.

Germanic traditions were often centered around fate, as this determined whether they would survive or fall victim to their enemy or the harsh environment they were surrounded by. Countless tales depict how the runes revealed fate or helped people alter it when needed. One of the tales showing how the runes helped alter a person's fate is also tied to their privilege as a writing tool. It comes from a period where only some people were skilled at rune carving, but many tried their chances with them. It begins with the great Viking Egil traveling across a farmer's land and learning that the farmer's child is very ill. In exchange for a meal, Egil offered to see if he could help the child. Upon entering the child's room, Egil noticed a piece of whalebone with rune carvings near the child's bed. Since he was versed in runic inscriptions, Egil learned that the runes on the whalebones (inscribed by someone who barely knew the runes) carried a negative message. He was sure that this caused the child to become ill. Egil replaced the whalebone with a piece of stone which contained a positive message, encouraging the child to recover - which they did.

Tales like the one above suggest a clear distinction between the different uses for the runes. Some runes were only meant to be used for communication, while others could be used for magical and other purposes. Despite this, some didn't respect this rule. Whether due to ignorance or malice, some still used the runes for inappropriate purposes. Followers of the ancient Norse traditions in modern times still claim that the different uses of the runes must be considered at all times. Beginners are advised to learn the meaning and association of each rule before attempting to use it - even for writing their names or simple messages.

The Meaning of Runes

The runes of the Elder Futhark have several meanings, and they're often open to the reader's interpretation. That said, here are the aspects of life each rune is associated with, along with their symbols and English equivalents. Their uses in magical practices will be discussed further on. However, you can also use them to translate short texts from English to Norse. For example, you can write your name or simple sentences. Keep in mind that the letters are not duplicated in the futhark. If you have the same letter twice in your name or the text you're trying to translate, you should only write the corresponding rune once.

Freyr's Aett

As the fertility god, Freyr is often associated with creativity, productivity, and the beginning of a new life. The runes in his aett reflect one's ability to create and find their place on the material plane.

ᚠ - Fehu

Fehu Rune.
https://pixabay.com/es/illustrations/fehu-runa-fe-runa-adivinaci%c3%b3n-6508602/

English equivalent: F

Pronounced "FAY-hoo," the name of this rune literally means cattle. However, in broad terms, it can also be translated to abundance, wealth, hope, property, luck, fortune, and material gain. It's also said to symbolize the fulfillment of foals and dreams in all aspects of life.

⋂- Uruz

Uruz Rune.
https://pixabay.com/es/illustrations/uruz-ur-runa-futhark-n%c3%b3rdico-6508604/

English equivalent: U

Pronounced "OO-rooz," Uruz in English means "wild ox." Like this magnificent animal, the rune is linked to the strength of will, courage, endurance, vitality, health, perseverance, and good times in general. It is believed that Uruz has the power to shape one's destiny through challenges.

Þ - Thurisaz

Thurisaz Rune.
https://pixabay.com/es/illustrations/thurisaz-jueves-runa-futhark-6508603/

English equivalent: Th

Pronounced "THUR-ee-sazh," this rune is translated as "giant" in English. It can also symbolize the hammer of Thor, protection, defense, disruptive forces, attack, or danger. Thurisaz means that you must change course and adopt a new one to harness divine power.

ᚠ - Ansuz

Ansuz Rune.
https://pixabay.com/es/illustrations/ansuz-runa-runas-futhark-2644294/

English equivalent: A

Pronounced "AHN-sooz," this rune means revelation. It is linked to Odin and his ability to communicate. It can also point toward other Norse deities who may send messages and insight through visions and signs. It's also said to illustrate mental capacity, the mouth, and organs needed for speech.

ᚱ - Raidho

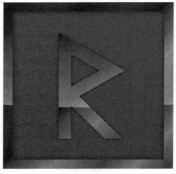

Raidho Rune.
https://pixabay.com/es/illustrations/raidho-runa-runas-futhark-2644605/

English equivalent: R

Pronounced "Rah-EED-ho," this rune is translated as a "journey on horseback." It can also signify any form of movement, progress in life, spiritual growth, the discovery of new perspectives, or the conscious decision to work for your goals and channel your energy for better results.

‹ - Kenaz

Kenaz Rune.
https://pixabay.com/es/illustrations/kenaz-runa-runas-futhark-2644856/

English equivalent: C / K

Pronounced "KEN-ahz," Kenaz is a Norse term for ulcer. It may also mean torch, transformation, passion, enlightenment, insight, or a purpose. Some believe the rune is the sight of receiving a higher calling towards following one's dreams. It's a sign that outside influences need to remain where they are.

X - Gebo

Gebo Rune.
https://pixabay.com/es/illustrations/gebo-runa-runas-futhark-2644831/

English equivalent: G

Pronounced "GHEB-o," this tune means "gift" in English. It's often referred to as a sign of gratitude or the need to exchange something through offerings. Gebo represents the way to obtain assistance, partnership, service, or luck through acts of generosity, charity, and providing what you expect in return.

ᛈ - Wunjo

Wunjo Rune.
https://pixabay.com/es/illustrations/wunjo-runa-runas-futhark-2644556/

English equivalent: W

Pronounced "WOON-yo," this rune represents joy and happiness. It may also mean the fulfillment of dreams and general well-being that may be threatened by an impending change. Wunjo brings destruction and tests one's strengths to see if one can maintain the ability to grow and thrive.

Heimdall's Aett

As the gatekeeper of the ancient gods, Heimdall ensures that only the ones able to show maturity and growth will prosper. His aett contains runes that lead to happiness through a journey of expansion and success.

ᚺ - Hagalaz

Hagalaz Rune.
https://pixabay.com/es/illustrations/hagalaz-runa-runas-futhark-2644694/

English equivalent: H

Pronounced "HA-ga-lah," this rune means "hail" in English. It represents difficulties that may halt plans or delay them at least. It may also refer to external input or the wrath of nature, which often has uncontrollable effects. It is said that Hagalaz can change one's life for the better.

ᚾ - Naudhiz

Naudhiz Rune.
https://commons.wikimedia.org/wiki/File:Runic_letter_naudiz.svg

English equivalent: N

Pronounced "NOWD-heez," Naudhiz is translated as "need." It can also mean resistance, distress, lacking, or difficulty thriving. However, in most cases, it symbolizes the necessity to overcome a challenge and manifest one's wishes and the ways to stop ignoring one's issues and unfulfilled desires.

I - Isa

Isa Rune.

English equivalent: I

Pronounced "EE-sa," this rune means "ice." It signals a sudden period of stillness when the world or a specific action must stop so you can see the changes you need to make. It's believed that Isa is needed for successful renewal. Otherwise, you'll keep following the same old patterns and remain stuck.

ᛃ - Jera

Jera Rune.

English equivalent: J / Y

Pronounced "YARE-a," Jera sounds very similar to its English translation - year. The appearance of this rune means harvest, rewards for hard work, life cycle, and conclusion of a period. At the same time, it also symbolizes new beginnings, opportunities for growth, and gathering abundance and wisdom.

ᛇ - Eihwaz

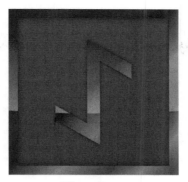

Eihwaz Rune.
https://pixabay.com/es/illustrations/eihwaz-runa-runas-futhark-2644633/

English equivalent: E / I

Pronounced "AY-wahz," this rune means "yew." As the symbol of ultimate wisdom, the yew tree represents uncovering the mysteries of life, finding inspiration, stability, the connection to the sacred wisdom and the divine. Eihwaz may also show you how to overcome a challenge through sacrifice.

ᛈ - Perthro

Perthro Rune.
https://pixabay.com/es/illustrations/perthro-runa-runas-futhark-2644941/

English equivalent: P

Pronounced "PER-thro," Perthro represents fate, prophecy, the occult, and mysticism. It may also mean fertility, self-awareness, and the chance to discover new ways to improve your fortune. When this rune appears, you can be sure that your future depends on your current choices.

ᛉ - Algiz

Algiz Rune.

English equivalent: Z

Pronounced "AL-geez," this rune means "elk." This animal is associated with good luck, courage, protection, and awakening. It signals that you must rely on your gut feelings to find the connection to your higher spiritual self. Algiz shows that your instincts are there to protect you.

ᛊ - Sowilo

Sowilo Rune.

English equivalent: S

Pronounced "So-WEE-lo," Sowilo means "sun" in English. This celestial body symbolizes solace, vitality, abundance, motivation, joy, and much more. Whatever challenge you may face, this rune provides reassurance that you'll persevere against them.

Tyr's Aett

Tyr, the powerful god of the skies, is the ultimate Norse symbol of war and justice. The runes in his aett refer to spiritual development and one's ability to create a legacy one can be proud of.

↑ - Tiwaz

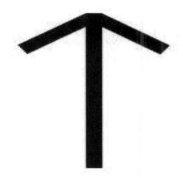

Tiwaz Rune.
https://commons.wikimedia.org/wiki/File:Runic_letter_tiwaz.png

English equivalent: T

Pronounced "TEE-wahz," this rune is translated as "the god Thor." It represents this deity's attributes, including bravery, leadership, honor, and strength. It can also mean making sacrifices for the greater good and thriving despite all challenges and difficulties.

ᛒ - Berkano

Berkano Rune.
https://pixabay.com/es/illustrations/berkana-runa-runas-futhark-2644529/

English equivalent: B

Pronounced "BER-Kah-no," Berkano means "birch," also linked to the birch goddess. It is associated with fertility, rebirth, and the beginning of a new project or relationship. The rune can also signal the potential for growth and find creative ways to begin anew or obtain sustenance.

ᛗ - Ehwaz

Ehwaz Rune.
https://pixabay.com/es/illustrations/ehwaz-runa-runas-futhark-2644896/

English equivalent: E

Pronounced "EH-wahz," this rune means "horse." In Norse mythology, this animal is the symbol of trust. Besides this, the rune may convey partnership, companionship, and faith in one's progress. It can also signify animal instinct, the need for assistance, or moving forward with your life.

ᛗ - Mannaz

Mannaz Rune
https://pixabay.com/es/illustrations/mannaz-runa-runas-futhark-2644241/

English equivalent: M

Pronounced "MAN-Naz," Mannaz is the rune for the English word "man." This means it represents humanity, mortality, and the balance between life and death. It's also believed to symbolize community and human traits like values and skills one develops throughout life.

⌐ - Laguz

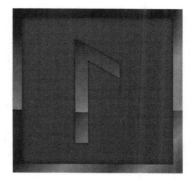

Laguz Rune.
https://pixabay.com/es/illustrations/laguz-runa-runas-futhark-2644773/

English equivalent: L

Pronounced "LAH-gooz," this rune has several meanings. Commonly linked to water and fluidity, potential, inner awareness, and the unknown. It also represents imagination, dreams, and ways to heal emotions by remaining open even through difficult times.

◇ - Ingwaz

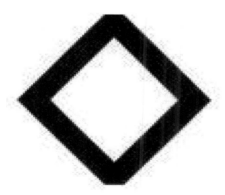

Ingwaz Rune.
https://commons.wikimedia.org/wiki/File:Runic_letter_ingwaz.png

English equivalent: Ng

Pronounced "ING-wahz," the name of this rune is linked to the god of Ingwaz. Its meaning varies from new beginnings to finding your potential through new energies, sexuality, family, ancestral wisdom, and more. It also represents peace and natural spiritual growth.

◊ - Othala

Othala Rune.

English equivalent: O

Pronounced "OH-tha-la," this rune means "inheritance." It's also linked to traditions, heritage, homecoming, inherent talents, nobility, ancestral wisdom, and property. It may also indicate that your values lie in your legacy and connection to Othala and your community.

⋈ - Dagaz

Dagaz Rune.

English equivalent: D

Pronounced "DAH-gahz," Dagaz is a Norse term for "day." It means hope, inspiration, the possibility of awakening, balance, significant changes at the beginning of the day, and the beginning of a new cycle. It can also signify happiness, clarity, spiritual growth, and self-consciousness.

Chapter 8: Working with Runes

As you've learned from the previous chapter, divination is one of the most prevalent uses of Norse runes. By the end of this chapter, you'll learn more about divinatory practices using the runic alphabet. You'll also receive several tips and formats for casting your own runic layouts and learning how to find answers to your own future-related questions.

Runes can be cast in several ways, either randomly or in a specific pattern.
https://www.pexels.com/photo/runic-letters-on-wood-chunks-and-ground-with-autumn-leaves-10110445/

Runic Divination

Looking into future outcomes with runes or rune casting is one of the easiest divinatory methods. Similarly to Tarot readings, the runes are laid or tossed on a flat surface and then interpreted. The runes can be cast in several ways, either randomly or in a specific pattern - with each rune having a specific purpose. Runic divination is used for answering simple questions to help you make a decision regarding your future. It's not fortune-telling, and it won't give you specific answers. The runes may reveal different influences related to your questions and answers. However, they'll never tell you a specific time of the day when something will happen. The runes represent the gateway to your subconscious - and by presenting their symbols in front of you, they'll guide you to find the answers that are already in your subconscious.

In ancient times, the runes were symbols carved on small sticks made from branches of nut-bearing trees. Traditionally, the runes were cast randomly on a piece of white cloth. The runecaster said a quick prayer to the gods or spirits they asked to help interpret the results and looked up to the sky while tossing the runes in front of them. They would then interpret the results according to their practices. Nowadays, you can buy runes in the form of small stones, rocks, bone, metal, or wooden objects with symbols carved or painted on them. Stones are typically the best options, as they are more durable, and there are fewer chances of rubbing the symbols off during use. You can even make these yourself, allowing you to form a stronger personal connection and charge them with your energy much more efficiently. That said, crafting your runes is a magical process that takes practice and knowledge. You may want to rehearse with some ready-made versions before committing to making your own. You can also buy crystal runes. These already come with powerful magic of their own, but you can infuse them with even more.

Casting the Runes

You can follow the ancient technique of tossing out the runes on a piece of white fabric or use some of the modern methods, such as laying them out on your altar (or a flat surface in your sacred space if you don't have an altar). It's recommended to face west while casting the runes, but if your practice requires you to face any other direction, you can do it that way. The method you opt for is a highly personal choice. Feel free to try whatever feels right. Keep your runes in a safe space, preferably in a pouch or box - which helps protect them from negative influences. Before you delve into any layouts, always cleanse your space, yourself, and your runes to ensure nothing will limit your ability to correctly interpret the answers.

Once you've dispelled any negative energy and prepared your mind and body for the reading, you can begin the casting. Put your hands into the container and mix your runes. Then, remove a number while formulating the appropriate question. It helps newbies consider the question even before you take out the runes. If needed, meditate on what you're interested in for 5-10 minutes before casting. Make sure you ask simple but specific questions. Try tossing one rune first and observing it as it lands. Has it landed face up or face down? Runes landing face up are the answer to the questions. Later, you can try casting three runes - these will also reveal the past and future influences related to your question. Traditionally, the runes were cast in odd numbers, and most modern layouts carried this approach.

Interpreting the Results

Since each rune has a different meaning, the results will always depend on how you interpret them. For example, Ansuz means "message." However, it can also mean inspiration, advice, or even enthusiasm. It's up to you to discern what this rune means to you under specific circumstances. You may improve your communication, seek advice on an important matter, or a new truth will be revealed to you in the future. You'll need to tap into your intuition to understand which answer is correct. While doing so, consider any future events, situations, or circumstances that Ansuz could apply. When could it come in handy? How could it help grow and prosper? Don't second guess whatever you see the answer to be. The first thing that comes to mind is typically the closest one to the answer you're looking for. If your gut tells you to seek advice on something, it is probably right.

Runes only provide hints and not exact answers. You'll need to hone your intuition and critical thinking abilities to learn how to interpret them correctly. You should also keep in mind that the future isn't fixed. When you change a single aspect that influences your future, the outcome will turn out differently from what you've predicted. This will happen no matter how precisely you've interpreted the answers in the present time. Anytime you change your thoughts and behavior, you're also changing your future. Practicing with the runes can be a great way to develop intuition. Besides teaching you how to shape your future to your liking, runic divination also promotes spiritual growth and happiness.

If you're tossing the runes, the interpretation also depends on the way they land. If you are just starting, you can choose to interpret only the ones that landed upright, as these provide more direct answers. Once you get the hang of it, you can try reading the ones that landed face down. These showcase hidden issues and truths. Like Tarot cards, Norse runes also have a reversed meaning when they land facing down.

Instead of focusing on the specifics, you should concentrate on the aspects of life the runes may be related to. Each rune showcases principles, events, and influences from different areas of life. By showing up when they do, they're trying to get your attention. The runes send a message through your intuition each time they appear, so make sure you listen to it. Of course, being able to do that requires plenty of introspection. This is where the spiritual side of runic divination comes in. Being a driving force for your intuition, this divinatory practice helps organize your thoughts and emotions. Apart from making you more focused and productive in your day-to-day life, this also leads to spiritual elevation. It helps you become more aware of your needs and desires and encourages you to make them a reality. In addition, the answers you receive during runic deviation may reveal hidden motivations and behavior patterns that aren't aligned with your values. It certainly gives you plenty to reflect on. Even if you aren't interested in achieving specific goals with the runes, working with them can be beneficial for your mental health and spiritual well-being.

Rune Layouts

Once you have practiced reading runes and made a connection with them, you can try casting simple layouts. Below are several spreads you can try interpreting, starting from the easy three-rune layout and ending with the complex 24-rune reading.

The Three-Rune Layout

Also called the Three Norns, this cast is great for beginners because there are few runes to interpret. You don't need to learn complicated patterns, either. Here is how to do it:

1. Place three runes in a horizontal line. They should be facing upwards.

2. The first rune on the left will tell you what past actions resulted in your present situation.

3. The middle rune illuminates the issues you are currently dealing with, which will help you better understand your current situation.

4. The last rune represents the most likely future outcome based on your actions and current situation.

The Four-Rune Spread

The four-rune cast (or Four Dwarves) is another easy layout that works for simple readings. It uses a circular pattern, and you'll read the runes going clockwise. Here is how to interpret this layout:

1. Take a deep breath, select four runes from your pouch, and lay them out in a circle. One should be on top, two in the middle, and one on the bottom.

2. The top rune symbolizes past events that caused you to be in your current situation.

3. The left rune in the middle points out any influence other people have on your current situation.

4. The right rune in the middle alludes to the present actions that affect your current situation.

5. The bottom rune characterizes the full scope of your situation - often revealing hidden truths, motivations, or anything else you weren't aware of or couldn't admit to yourself.

The Five-Rune Layout

This cast is similar to the previous one, except you'll lay out the runes in the shape of a cross. It also uses two more symbols which means you may get a more in-depth answer to your questions. Here is how to cast it:

1. After relaxing, place five runes forming a cross. Start interpreting them from the bottom.

2. The rune at the base of the cross alludes to general influences related to your question.

3. The rune at the left horizontal side of the cross indicates the impact of negative forces related to the outcome in question.

4. The rune at the right horizontal side of the cross represents a short answer to your question.

5. The rune at the top of the cross hints at the positive energies that will impact the outcome.

6. The rune in the middle symbolizes any future actions that will impact the answer to your question.

The Seven-Rune Spread

When you gain confidence in reading simple layouts, you can move on to interpret more complex casts. The seven-rune cast can answer specific questions and reveal truths you weren't even aware of. Here is how to cast it:

1. Take a deep breath, clear your mind, and lay out seven runes (face-up) in a V form. Start interpreting from the top left side.

2. The top left rune indicates past influences that may impact the answer to the question.

3. The second rune from the left illuminates how your current actions may affect the answer to the question.

4. The last rune on the bottom left alludes to future influences that may impact the answer to the question.

5. The rune at the bottom of the V points to the actions you should take to reach the desired outcome.

6. The first rune on the right side at the bottom indicates any emotions that may impact your actions.

7. The rune above the previous one indicates any challenges related to the question.

8. The rune in the highest position on the right side represents the most likely future result related to your questions.

Nine-Rune Cast

In Norse mythology, nine is the number that holds answers to a lot of questions. This cast uses nine runes, but you won't have to worry about laying them out in a specific pattern. You'll just toss them out and see where they land. Here is how to cast and interpret runes with this method:

1. Take a deep breath and reach into your rune bag or box while focusing on your question.

2. Take out nine runes and place them in your dominant hand.

3. Closing your eyes, scatter the runes in front of you

4. Open your eyes and observe the positions of the runes after landing.

5. See how many runes are facing up and how many have landed face down. The latter indicates problems you weren't aware of. Despite this, they may affect your future. The ones facing you are influences you were already aware of.

6. Take a look at the runes that landed close to the center of the surface you're working on - these are the most important influences you need to focus on. The ones closer to the edge are less important but should not be disregarded either.

The 24-Rune Layout

Also called the Runic Year, this spread is typically used for long-term planning. Casting at the beginning of the year allows you to see an entire year's worth of influences and possible events and issues you may face in the coming year. It requires a bit more preparation in terms of cleansing - and you'll need to focus more as there is a lot more information to interpret. Here is how to cast this spread:

1. Lay out the 24 runes in a 3x8 grid, and start reading from the right side of the first row.

2. The first rune in the first row indicates the ways you'll obtain financial gains and prosperity.

3. The second rune represents the ways you can attain physical health and fitness.

4. The third rune shows how you'll defend yourself or destroy any issues on your way.

5. The fourth rune hints towards obtaining wisdom and motivation to keep going.

6. The fifth rune illuminates the direction of your life's path as seen under the current influences.

7. The sixth rune represents the knowledge you'll gain through the year.

8. The seventh rune shows what skills you can develop and hone and the gifts you'll receive.

9. The last rune in the first row alludes to how you'll obtain peace, harmony, and joy in your life.

10. The first rune on the right side of the second row indicates future changes that may await you.

11. The second rune represents the action you must take to obtain the desired results.

12. The third rune will show any obstacles that may hinder you on your journey.

13. The fourth rune indicates success and achievements you'll gain throughout the year.

14. The fifth rune alludes to challenging situations and choices you'll need to make to overcome them.

15. The sixth rune illuminates the inner skills that you need to work on.

16. The seventh rune symbolizes crucial life situations you'll find yourself in.

17. The last rune of the second row brings forward the inner energy that'll guide you.

18. The first rune on the right side of the third row represents legal and business affairs.

19. The second rune shows how you'll obtain prosperity and growth.

20. The third rune indicates the friendships and other relationships you'll form.

21. The fourth rune symbolizes your expected social status in the coming year.

22. The fifth rune alludes to the changes in your emotional state.

23. The sixth rune represents any romantic or sexual relationships you'll have.

24. The seventh rune shows how you'll obtain balance in all areas of life.

25. The last rune of the bottom row symbolizes all the assets you'll gain throughout the year.

Using Casting Boards

If you want answers to specific questions but aren't sure which cast would work the best, another option is to use a casting board. These are pre-made sheets or boards with areas of the present, past, future, and other crucial aspects of your life already laid out. All you need to do is toss the runes and look where they land. The ones that land in the past section will give you answers related to your past experiences. The ones landing in the present section are linked to your present, while the ones in the future will reveal what you should expect moving forward.

Chapter 9: Celtic Shamanism and Druidry

This chapter covers everything you need to know about Celtic Shamanism and Druidry. Here, you'll find out what each term means and understand the core beliefs of each practice. You'll understand the roles of shamans and druids and come across a section that illustrates the difference between both spiritual philosophies.

Druidic Ceremony for the Autumn Equinox on Primrose Hill in London, England.
Simon King, CC BY-SA 4.0 <https://creativecommons.org/licenses/by-sa/4.0>, via Wikimedia Commons:
https://commons.wikimedia.org/wiki/File:Druids_on_Primrose_Hill_Autumn_Equinox.jpg

Celtic Shamanism

Celtic Shamanism studies the spiritual beliefs and practices of ancient Irish, Welsh, Scottish, and some English people. Celtic people belonged to a large, diversified tribe that resided in the area around Germany and encompassed the French Gauls around the year 1500 BC.

Asia Minor was thought to be the origin of these indigenous tribes before they spread out toward eastern and western Europe, the Celtic Isles, and the Iberian peninsula. Ancient Celts were mostly known for their trading and mining skills. Germany's salt mines and France's gold mines largely contributed to their prominence and wealth.

These tribes were war-like yet open-minded. They had no problem taking over the lands they came across while traversing Europe. Still, they didn't mind being influenced by the artistic expressions and spiritual beliefs of others.

Shamanism isn't an organized religious tradition. It can be thought of as a way of life that requires you to journey your way into the spiritual realm and back so you can connect with your spirit guides and ask for their guidance on several matters, including healing and divination. There is no particular text that you can turn to when practicing Shamanism. It's important to understand that even though all practitioners share the same core beliefs, their shamanic practices, rituals, spiritual journeys, and experiences can greatly differ.

One of the core aspects of Shamanism is that its practitioners believe that everything around them has a spirit. They thought that the entire world was interconnected and that the spirit realm stimulated our world. Shamans trust that they can refer to the spiritual world whenever they need to ask for protection, wisdom, or healing. Even when Christianity made its way into Europe, people still believed that the divine was eminent in all aspects of nature.

Who Are Shamans?

A shaman is someone who journeys into the realm of the spirit as a proxy for wisdom and healing-related advice that would help them and those around them. Shamans had a broad range of skills that benefited the community in numerous ways.

For instance, a ban feasa/leighis, which translates to "woman of knowledge/healing," conducted healing rituals, broke evil spells, eliminated unwanted spirits, and offered healing remedies. The healing work of those who followed the faery faith was dedicated to the fae and inspired by it.

Omen hunters and seers traditionally conducted oracle work to inform people about the future. They also determined the wisdom behind some of the community's decisions and actions. Unlike the modern-day world, storytellers and poets were not regarded as entertainment figures but played significant societal roles. They were even regarded as healers. After all, art, in all its forms, is meant to leave an impact on our mental and emotional states.

A Shaman's Worldview

A shaman's worldview is characterized by its depth. They experience the world differently than we do because their perceptions are far more layered and analytical. They listen deeply and actively to everything around them. They're avid observers of nature and always live in the present moment. They don't concern themselves much with the past, and even though they are blessed with the gift of divination, they don't spend a lot of time worrying about the future. Shamans make the most of each moment that they're living, making it their mission to experience it with all their senses.

They acknowledge nature's beauty and express gratitude for everything they have. Being engrossed and attentive to nature and the current moment allows them to feel thankful for the things that we deem normal or insignificant. We get caught up in the dynamics of the everyday world that we take phenomena like the rising sun, streaming rivers, and animal produce for granted. Shamans, however, greet the sun each morning. They thank the plants and animals for sustaining them and honor them for keeping them warm and cooking their food. They end their day with a thankful prayer to nature.

Shamans garner their strength from this humbled, acknowledging, and thankful attitude. They realized that these simple gestures meant a lot to nature and the divine. Since they believed that spirit existed in everything, it was only appropriate for them to pay their respects and grant it their attention at all times.

A Celtic shaman's universe comprises three realms: the lower world, the middle world, and the upper world. They believed all of them were conjoined by the Tree of Life. This tree's roots are deeply planted into the lower world. Its trunk extends through the middle world, where we exist, and into the upper realm. The branches of this great tree are responsible for keeping the sun, the stars, and the moon up in the sky.

They believe that when they transcend into the realm of the divine, they climb up the tree or the great ladder. There resides the Great Mother goddess, deities, spirits, the stars, and other celestial bodies. They can also make their way into the lower realm by climbing down the roots of the tree where there are the spirits of fire and the earth and the horned one. He is the deity of the underworld and the protector of all animals.

Despite the size of the realms and the great Tree of Life, shamans believed that they all exist within a hazelnut shell that lies next to the source of all the wisdom in the world: the Well of Segais.

Celtic Shamans and Shapeshifting

Shapeshifting is another core aspect of the Celtic shamanic practice. This spiritual experience is essentially about the ability to simultaneously exist and partake in several realities. Shamans also believe that shapeshifting into another animal or living being allows them to draw on their healing and guiding powers. Their journey is considered incomplete if they're unable to move their consciousness into that of another being before returning.

Celtic Shamans and Totem Beasts

According to Celtic shamanic beliefs, everyone is protected by a totem beast that accompanies them on their life journey at the time of birth. This totem animal can stay with a person until they die. Shamanic practitioners obtain other power animals, in addition to their totem animals, at different times during their life. These animal guides may join a shaman at their own will or can be called upon for help. Sometimes, practitioners draw upon the animal's powers, whether it is their intuition, strength, sharp senses, or speed. In other cases, the animals tell the practitioner things they can't discern independently.

During the earlier years of human existence, animals and humans were much closer on several levels than they are today. We used to live in closer proximity to animals, and there was a higher level of mutual understanding. As the world grew more modernized, we fell out of touch with nature and the animal kingdom. Shamans, however, are keen on maintaining strong relationships with animals because numerous spirits represent them in the world of the divine.

Druidry

There are prominent similarities between Wicca and Paganism. However, it's important to remember that Druidism is not a subset of Wicca. Some Wiccans choose to practice Druidism, too, because of the similarities they share. The majority of Druids, however, are not Wiccan.

There are few reliable written accounts about Druidry. Most of the information that modern practitioners know comes from Celtic lore, mythology, and legend. They also rely on the academic information offered by historians and anthropologists as it serves as a basis for their practices, rituals, and rites.

Druidry, like Shamanism, is a nature-based belief system. Although it is very similar to Wicca, it focuses more on nature and ancestry. Druidry doesn't have a scripture or a sacred book to turn to. This is why it can come in several forms and easily adapt to various spiritual beliefs. Many people don't realize that regardless of your faith, whether you're a monotheist, polytheist, animist, or pantheist, you can still adopt some aspects of the druid philosophy.

Monotheistic druids believe in a single deity, while polytheists affirm the deities. Animistic and pantheistic druids may not believe in the presence of a single God. However, they would still affirm his existence as a force that exists in everything around us.

Druidism is incredibly tolerant of various spiritual and philosophical beliefs. The best thing about it is that it teaches that no belief system is superior to another. It all depends on the path that the individual chooses to follow.

The following are the core elements of the Druid faith:

- Life is a journey. All the stages of life, such as birth, adulthood, marriage, children, and all the stages leading up to death, and death itself, create a journey.

- Druidry is a healing practice. Healing utilizes holistic methods to heal the mind, body, and spirit.

- Druidry is a magical practice. It involves the use of divination practices to foretell the future and allows us to manifest our ideas.

- Reincarnation is possible. Ancient druids believed in a type of reincarnation which involved the journeying of the soul to the Otherworld before its reincarnation. This was taught in both animal and human forms and is still held onto by some modern practitioners.

- Each person must unlock their potential. Unlocking our potential is necessary if we wish to develop our intuitive, creative, intellectual, and psychic powers.

- All life is sacred. All life is equally valuable and sacred and withholds aspects of divinity. Animals, plants, and humans are all of the same levels of importance.

- We need to be in touch with nature. Practicing Druidry keeps us aligned with our ancestors, natures, and, ultimately, ourselves.

- There is an Otherworld. There is an otherworld that we will transcend to when we die. Although this place exists beyond our consciousness, it can be accessed via visualization, meditation, or other techniques that trigger a trance state.

Even though Christianity replaced Druidry in the 7th century, some British people found inspiration in this philosophy during the 18th century. There was very little information about ancient sages and practitioners; however, this spiritual practice was somehow rekindled. It didn't take long before other scholars around Europe also found the subject appealing.

Those who take up an interest in Druidry are often individuals who grow discontented with conventional belief systems. They wish to build a deeper connection with their ancestors and the earth on which they live. People who seek comfort in Druidry are those who wish to feel rooted and grounded in an incredibly fast-paced world. Druidry, for many people, serves as an anchor.

Who Are Druids?

A druid can be loosely defined as a member of the educated ancient Celtic society. They took up various societal roles, including teaching, priesthood, and acting as judges. Many of them were also scientists and philosophers. They seldom recorded their activities, so very little information about them is known.

Druids were considered the official arbitraries of justice and the truth because they studied moral philosophy. They were trusted enough to make decisions that would serve the greater good of society. They preached the concepts of the afterlife and the existence of an Otherworld. Druids developed solar and lunar calendars and studied the movement of celestial objects. Their understanding of the world prompted their celebration of the 8 annual Sabbats, which were seasonal celebrations.

It would take someone around 20 years of studying to become a druid. All the information they needed to know was transmitted orally. Since there were no books or notes to study, the whole learning process relied on memory.

Their role in the community was similar to that of priests now. They aimed to help people build a connection with the divine. Druids were highly esteemed members of the community. Their powers didn't only encompass spiritual practices, but they also had authority over the public. They were able to banish those who failed to conform to sacred laws. The Druids were powerful enough to call off wars. They didn't have to become army men, nor were they charged tax payments either. Druid women were equally esteemed and rightful. They were able to call their marriages off and serve in the army if they desired.

Julius Caesar, one of the primary sources of information about the Druids, explained that the Druids executed public and private sacrifices. They mainly sacrificed criminals for those who fell very ill or were in danger of dying in battle. However, they would sometimes sacrifice innocent individuals if the situation called for it.

They also advised those who went to them for guidance, judged all quarrels in the community, and decreed appropriate penalties. Caesar recounted that those who failed to meet the decree were exempted from sacrifice, which was thought to be a harsh punishment. The Druids appointed a chief, who was replaced upon death. They voted between candidates if there were several equally qualified ones. That said, they often thought that they wouldn't be able to come to a satisfactory resolution without armed violence.

The Bards

Bards were responsible for keeping and reinforcing traditions. They were thought to be the protectors of the world's sacredness. They weren't as thoroughly educated as Druids, as they likely only completed the first level of apprenticeship training. That said, they weren't at all thought to be inferior to Druids.

Bards could achieve different levels of accomplishment. Of course, the most proficient ones were treated with the highest regard. They also filled in several roles of the Druid and the Ovate. Ovates were mainly seers and diviners but were also possibly midwives, herbalists, and healers.

Training as a Bard was not an easy feat. It was a challenging and lengthy process that took around 12 years.

Celtic Shamanism vs. Druidry

Both shamans and druids were highly respected members of society. Shamans were considered diviners, healers, and proxies between the human world and the spiritual realm. Druids were regarded as diviners, healers, political advisors, and religious leaders. While modern-day practitioners of both philosophies have the same skill sets, they contribute to society differently.

The main difference between Shamanism and Druidry is that the former can be described as a worldview or approach, while the latter is considered a religion for many people.

The word "shaman" has recently evolved to describe any person who interacts with the world of spirit despite their faith or religion. The Druidic philosophy, however, is a nature-oriented spiritual system. This means that a person can be a Druid or a shaman. Even if they're not necessarily practitioners of Celtic Shamanism, they may supplement their druidic practices with shamanic activities and rituals.

Here's a rundown of the core beliefs of both practices:

- Animism is among the core aspects of Shamanism. Practitioners believe that each entity in nature has a spirit that you can interact with. While some of them are quite helpful, others are malicious. Druids are also animists. This nature-centered practice revolves around believing that nature has its own divine spirit.

- Shamans believe in a non-ordinary reality, which is the existence of another realm for the spirits. They embark on shamanic journeys to transcend into the world of spirit for various reasons, including holistic healing and divination.

- Shamans think that 3 realms make up an extraordinary world. Druids believe in the existence of a similar place (particularly to the upper world): the Otherworld. Since they believe in an afterlife, they think this is where humans go after death. However, this place can also be accessed by inducing a trance state or with the help of meditation.

- Shamans and druids both believe in interconnection. They think that all living beings are connected and are, therefore, in touch with the world of spirit.

Celtic Shamanism and Druidry have numerous aspects in common. While both of these philosophies share, more or less, the same core beliefs, they are not mutually exclusive. Celtic Shamanism is considered a methodology or approach. It has expanded to take on a broader meaning. Anyone who interacts with the world of spirit, regardless of their religion, is now regarded as a shaman by many.

Druidry, on the other hand, is more of a religion or belief system. That said, it is very tolerant of various spiritual and philosophical beliefs. It can also be adapted to numerous faiths, whether the practitioner is monotheistic, polytheistic, or animistic. There aren't many reliable written accounts about Druidry. Most of what we know comes from Julius Caesar's accounts, Celtic lore, and mythology. This is perhaps because the Druid learning process relied on memory and the oral transmission of information.

Chapter 10: Walking the Druid Path

In this chapter, you'll find out how you can become a druid and what it means to be one. You'll also learn everything you need to know about practicing Druidry in today's world. Finally, you'll find an exercise that can help you enrich your Druidic experience as a new practitioner.

Many druids commit to this spiritual path by going off the grid.

PicturePrince, CC BY-SA 4.0 <https://creativecommons.org/licenses/by-sa/4.0>, via Wikimedia Commons: https://commons.wikimedia.org/wiki/File:Croome_Park_Worcs_Druid_statue_1.jpg

How Can One Become a Druid?

Druidry is essentially a journey of a deep, observant relationship with everything you encounter. Every day, we come in contact with nature, people, and animals. Some people come in contact with other unworldly entities too. However, suppose we're talking about the terrestrial plane. In that case, we deal with the land and other living beings and how we fit into this complex. Becoming a druid in ancient times took around 20 years. However, modern druids now believe that one can get into this belief system by growing their awareness and learning to be fully present in the current moment.

Understanding how your life positively and negatively contributes to the balance and well-being of the ecosystem is a great step forward. Druidry is a nature-centered religion, which is why druids try to keep their carbon footprint as small as possible. While avoiding all environmentally harmful activities in today's world is impossible, you should always seek less damaging and greener alternatives.

Many druids commit even further to this spiritual path by going off the grid. They grow their own food, engage in recycling and composting activities, make their own tools or clothes, and purchase second-hand items. Some believe that the world is overpopulated, so they refuse to have children.

Those who don't live off the grid try their best to make appropriate and good use of technology. They try to positively influence the community in which they live by promoting helpful, sustainable, ethical, and honorable practices.

One person may decide to completely boycott carbon-fueled transportation by choosing to walk or bike instead. They resort to modern means of transportation only if they really need to. Another person may think that living like that doesn't suit their lifestyle. They may work far from home, travel frequently, or run several errands a day. In that case, a druid will aim to use technology as mindfully as possible. They understand the consequences that come with technological advancements but still realize that avoiding these improvements isn't practical in today's fast-paced world. Despite their different approaches, each individual has an aware, personal, and mindful relationship with the world around them. Neither person is a better druid than the other.

There isn't a particular strict code or detailed guide to live by. Druidry adapts to various living conditions and rapid technological and societal changes. Each druid leads a unique life and practices their faith in a way that feels true to them. While not all druids have the same way of life, the core elements and beliefs of Druidry unify them.

Connections and Values

Practitioners are always on an ongoing quest to cultivate a deep spiritual bond and empathetic connections with their direct environment, the world, the entire universe, and all realities. They often find their deities where they least expect them, get to know their names, and build a transcendental, deep relationship with them. Each person comes in contact with their gods differently because there are almost no written records of ancient Druid practices. Most of what we know today is based on trial and error, intuition, and generational telltales. This is why any relationship that a person builds with a deity is incredibly personal. No one can tell you how to go about your faith or how to believe. You must lean into your intuition and do whatever feels right to you.

To be a druid, for many, is to have a voice and be heard. Many people use their faith as an opportunity to stand up for their principles and what they think is right. Most druids participate in eco-protest and activism-related activities. They always try to create positive changes in the world and contribute to a better living environment for all living beings.

Druidry is a vivacious and celebratory religion. It is ritualistic and connection-based. It's important that in your strife to build strong connections with the Earth and the realm of the spirits, you don't forget to cultivate equally deep relationships with those around you. If there's a Druid community in your area, don't pass up on the opportunity to meet up with them during celebrations, rituals, and even casual meet-ups. If there aren't any Druids nearby, you should still aim to interact with people who share the same values and interests. You can join clean-ups, charity events, and other volunteer work.

Awen

Awen can either be chanted silently within the soul or out loud. It comprises 3 sounds:

1. Ah makes you feel purposeful, incites joy, and promotes creativity and power.

2. Oo enlarges and maintains the power and energy that you have embraced, encouraging it to flourish.

3. Enn brings the whole process to an end. It builds boundaries and serves as a containment. It paves the way for everything that ah and oo have inspired and instigated.

Learning how to open yourself up to Awen is not a challenging feat. Pretend it's a window- how would you let all the natural air and light in? You'll probably approach the window, unhinge its latch, and open it wide. That's the only thing you need to do to let the sunshine, wind, and fresh air flow inside. They do all the work for you: light up your home, renew the air inside, and cool down and freshen up the room. You just sit back and watch it all unfold. It's exactly the same with Awen. You only need to take the first step to open it up and embrace it so you can allow it to do its thing without any interference.

Druidry lives up to the magic of the term itself. It encourages everyone who practices any art form to work in harmony to celebrate the Awen. Awen is a term that celebrates spirit, vitality, inspiration, and energy.

Reading into fables, parables, and telltales like the Mabinogion and the Tales of Taliesin can give you insight into the heritage of Druidry. You can learn about how people communicated with deities, related to them, celebrated them, and worked with them to achieve certain purposes pre-Druidry. You'll come to see that despite the fact that other spiritual beliefs influenced it with stories that have been recorded for hundreds of years, Druidry was unique because of how it allowed practitioners to adapt it to their needs. It never becomes dated because each generation revamps it to fit the standards of their world by keeping the core value intact. Its oral nature allows for a sense of continuity over the ages.

In a Nutshell

The question still stands- "How do you become a Druid?"

If you want to become a Druid, you must make peace with the fact that there is no solid answer to this question. While Druidry comes with no sacred book that you can turn to for guidance, there are many things you can do to build your own identity as a Druid. Reading books, such as this one, getting to know other Druids, partaking in rituals, connecting with nature, understanding the core beliefs of Druidry, reaching out to the divine and your spirit guides, learning how to become nature-centered, and most importantly, leading with your personal morals and values are all things that can help you out.

You may wonder at which stage of your practice it becomes okay to identify as a Druid. You must realize that no matter how much knowledge you have, you'll never know everything there is to know about this belief system- there is always something to learn. In other words, becoming a self-identified Druid is not necessarily tied to the amount of information you have obtained. Instead, it has to do with how deeply connected you are to the divine and the belief itself. Once you feel like you can formulate your own (non-judgmental) opinions on other people's practices and Druidic way of life, you'll be able to build your own identity as a practitioner.

Modern Druidry

The basics of Druid practices are shared by all practitioners and serve as a good foundation for developing personal practice-related standards, beliefs, morals, and ethics. Modern Druids are encouraged to seek the truth above all else.

Druidry today differs significantly from ancient practices, particularly because most of what we know today is based on observations, generational stories, and archaeological evidence and interpretations. Back then, practitioners didn't have access to as much information and tools as we do today, which is why their practices were purely experimental. However, nowadays, we have scholastic proof of natural phenomena, which further authenticates the Druidic experience. While many aspects of the belief system remain purely spiritual and intuitive, others have become fact-based. This makes Druidry more relatable and easier to wrap one's head around, especially for those who are still new to the practice. That said, many people prefer to turn a blind eye to the facts when it comes to spiritual beliefs and religion. They feel it's only right to let their intuition, the universe, and their spirit guides steer them toward the truth.

Roman recounts of ancient Druidic practices are highly illegal and unacceptable in today's world. Human sacrifices, for instance, is an activity that raises numerous questions. Did they sacrifice innocent people or execute dangerous criminals? It is believed that they were popular for keeping the heads of their enemies as trophies. Was this a sacrificial act or a prideful practice? Regardless of the truth behind this gruesome practice, human sacrifice is insufferable in today's world.

Upon exploring ancient Druidic practices, you could easily tell that everything they did was aligned with their time. They were exposed to numerous cultures and traditions and had to settle on trade agreements. They were also entangled in political issues, as they served as advisors to the rulers. They also healed the ill using more advanced tools and medical techniques than the Romans were capable of- they were truly ahead of their time! Druids helped their communities in numerous aspects, serving as teachers, judges of the truth, lawmakers, and ritual leaders, and advocated for great causes.

They also promoted positive practices and social and environmental welfare and acted as counselors and spiritual service providers.

Modern Practices

Most Druids today are polytheistic. They believe in the existence of various deities, which mainly belong to the Welsh or Irish pantheons. The majority of practitioners work with Celtic pantheons. However, some groups believe that it's fine to follow whichever Indo-European pantheon they see fit, including Norse, Russian, and Germanic ones. It's commonly believed that some deities are not meant to be worked with for specific purposes. They'll choose the right god or goddess to work with, depending on the situation at hand. They often refer to a correspondence chart to ensure that they make the right choice. While many pagans worship a different deity each week, druids don't believe in this practice. This is because many pagan belief systems view all deities as a subset of a single divine figure, while Druids think each deity has its own individual identity. Since Druidry can be adapted to each person's faith, some Christians are also druids who believe in a single god. Others believe in no deities at all. They just adopt Druidry as mere philosophy.

One of the best things about Druidry is that it's open to everyone. It doesn't matter what your faith or ethnicity is. You are always welcome to explore Druidic practices. It's worth mentioning, however, that some modern druids choose to be very exclusive with their rituals and Druidic practices. They'll want to get to know you before they let you in on their spiritual activities.

Magic workings are not an essential aspect of Druidic practices. Wiccans prefer to practice magic because they view it as an opportunity to sharpen their skills. It is, more or less, a major part of their spiritual practice. However, many modern Druids never cast spells, and this doesn't make them any less of a true druid. Since nature is a quintessential part of Druidry, Neo-druids always do their best to choose more environmentally-friendly options.

There are 8 popular seasonal Pagan festivals: Samhain, Yule, Imbolc, Ostara, Beltane, Litha, Lughnassadh, and Mabon. However, only 4 of them are actually Celtic: Samhain, Imbolc, Beltane, and Lughnassadh. Even though many Druids like to celebrate all Sabbats or festivals, most of them choose to celebrate only the 4 main Celtic ones. Keep in mind that some druids are also part of spiritual groups that require them to celebrate all 8 Sabbats.

Modern druids aim to serve their needs, community, and deities by partaking in community services and volunteer work. They also practice ecological awareness, make environmentally-friendly decisions, strive to maintain balance in all aspects of their lives, and maintain respectful and consistent spiritual practices. Individuals who only view Druidry as a philosophy tend to approach their personal religions with a Druid approach.

Enrich Your Druidic Experience

Here are some things you can do to enrich your Druidic experience, even if you're still just starting out:

Go Outside

Disconnect from technology for a day and go outside. Go for a walk in a nature-dense place and find a quiet place to stay in. If you live in the city, visit your local park. This will not be like any other walk you've had- it is a walk with a purpose. Think about the last walk you had. What were you thinking about? Your mind was probably busy with thoughts about your to-do list, financial problems, family issues, or work. Leave your baggage behind for this walk. Only focus on the present moment and fully engage in the experience.

Observe

Once you find your quiet place, you must refine your senses. Extend your arms to your sides, creating the shape of a T. Look straight, right above the horizon, while moving your arms back. Move your fingers around while moving your arms forward again. Keep your arms still but allow your fingers to wiggle when they come into your peripheral vision. Keep looking straight ahead. This is something known as Wide Angle Vision. Once you see your fingers while your arms are extended to your sides, slowly drop your arms down while keeping your attention on everything around you.

Hear

Move your hands again and place them behind your ears. You'll be using them to control your hearing. Keeping your hands behind your ear can help you hear things more effectively. Focus on what you can hear better. Stay in this position for a while before moving your hands away. Listen to everything around you. You'll likely hear layers of sound that you didn't know you could hear. Listen mindfully, and then try to combine this exercise with the "observe" one.

Smell

Take some grass from the ground and crunch it in your palms. Take several sniffs in short, quick bursts, and avoid taking long ones. You can also try doing this exercise with soil or tree twigs around you. Try sniffing the air in short and quick bursts, as well. Then, combine this exercise with the heart and observe. Focusing on all three senses simultaneously can be very challenging. However, you'll master it through practice.

Each Druid decides how they will put their spiritual beliefs into practice. However, all modern-day practitioners can agree on the importance of living up to a certain level of integrity at all times. They also actively seek their personal truth through embarking on their own educational journeys, learning from other people, ritualistic practices, connecting with nature, and meditating.

Appendix: A-Z of Pagan Symbols

Pagan traditions are full of symbolism. This chapter serves as an appendix for the most used and significant ancient and modern symbols.

Aegishjalmur

This symbol is also known as the Helm of Awe. It is the epitome of safety and power, and its symbol resembles a circle that includes 8 staves. Fafnir, Hreidmar's son, carried this symbol with him when he fought Siegfried in the form of a dragon. Even though most of the dragon's power came from the Helm of Awe, Siegfried won the battle before taking the Aegishjalmur for himself.

Viking warriors used to draw this emblem on their foreheads because they believed it would strike fear in the hearts of their enemies and help protect them in battle. Besides being a protective symbol, the Helm of Awe was also thought to boost one's mental and physical strength.

Ankh

This is perhaps the most renowned ancient Egyptian emblem. It is popularly known as the Key of Life and was adopted in Paganism and Christianity as an emblem of the afterlife, eternity, life, and rebirth. Christians started using this symbol in the 4th and 5th AD after Egypt's partial Christianization.

Air

According to alchemy, air is one of the 4 basic elements on Earth. Pagans adopted the Alchemical symbol of air, which is an upward-facing triangle with a horizontal line cutting through its upper half. Since air is a necessity for human existence, it serves as an emblem of all life-giving forces and the soul itself. Pagans typically include it in spiritual practices and rituals.

Earth

The alchemical symbol of Earth is a downward-facing triangle with a horizontal line cutting through its lower (pointed) half. It symbolizes mother nature and is an emblem of physical movements, fertility, abundance, and nature.

Eye of Horus

Horus was the ancient Egyptian god of healing and protection. His eye was particularly known to be a protective symbol. It was believed to be extremely powerful, and ancient Egyptians trusted it would keep them safe in life-threatening situations. They sent it off with fishermen to protect them from the raging seas and buried it with those who had passed or drew it on their coffins to keep them safe on their journey to the afterlife. The pagans added the Eye of Horus to their symbols and incorporated the correspondent ancient Egyptian traditions into their lives.

Fire

The alchemical symbol of fire is a regular, upward-facing triangle. Fire is believed to be the embodiment of masculinity. Even though it can be destructive, it is also a life-supporting force since we need it to stay warm and cook food. Fire is also a symbol of intense emotions, like love, passion, and anger.

Hecate's Wheel

This symbol is the emblem of the Hecate. She is the Greek deity of magic and the moon. This wheel is representative of the Triple Goddess' three aspects, which are representative of the different phases in a woman's life. Each of them has distinct Wiccan practices. Pagans use this symbol to attract prosperity. Since the emblem is in the shape of a labyrinth, it is also believed to symbolize renewal and rebirth.

Mjolnir

Mjolnir, which is known as Thor's hammer in pop culture, is another Norse pagan symbol. Thor, the god of thunder, is among the most prominent Norse mythology figures. It was believed that when Thor threw Mjolnir, it always hit the right target and came flying right back to him. Viking warriors wore the symbol on necklaces because it was associated with protection. Thor's hammer remained a significant aspect of Norse culture even after the emergence of Christianity. Mjolnir is also popular among those who follow the neopagan religion of Asatru. Pagans even used the symbol to bless marriages.

Ouroboros

Depicted as a snake eating its own tail, Ouroboros is also known as the infinity symbol. This emblem is significant to various cultures, making it among the most important symbols to the entirety of humankind. Cleopatra the Alchemist (not Egypt's Ptolemaic ruler) is considered to be the first to use this symbol. Her works date back to the 3rd Century BC.

Cleopatra featured the Ouroboros in a work that revolved around the mythical philosopher's stone, which was thought to turn any metal into pure gold. Many alchemists used the infinity symbol to represent life, death, and rebirth, which is the unending cycle of life. It was also associated with Mercury, the chemical element, rebirth, and reincarnation. The Ouroboros also represents the harmony and duality of two opposing forces or sides.

Pentacle

A pentacle is a five-pointed star enclosed in a circle. According to pagan beliefs, circles symbolize power and infinity. In that case, the circle in the Pentacle reinforces the power of the five-pointed star. It also reflects the interconnectedness of earth, air, water, fire, and spirit. Pagans use this emblem for protection in their practices.

Pentagram

This symbol looks exactly like a pentacle. However, it isn't enclosed in a circle. The 5 points of the star represent the 4 basic elements plus the spirit.

Septogram

The Septogram is a seven-pointed star. The symbol is also known as the faery star, heptagram, and septagram. Besides Paganism, this emblem is significant in other faiths, like Christianity and Islam, across the globe. Christians use it as an emblem for the creation of the world, which took 7 days, while Muslims use it to symbolize the Quran's first 7 verses. The heptagram in Paganism is associated with numerous concepts that come in 7s. For example, it was used to represent 7 ancient classical planets and the Seven Sisters or Pleiades, which were thought to be the titan Atlas' daughters.

Svefnthorn

Norse witches and magicians used the Svefnthorn to induce sleep among their subjects. This symbol was also known as the Sleep Thorn, and its depiction differs from one source to the other.

The Horned God

The Horned God represents masculinity, hunting, and sexuality. It is symbolized by a circle that has an upward-facing crescent on top of it. It's used in Wiccan invocation rituals, particularly ones that have to do with fertility.

The Sacred Spiral

The Sacred Spiral was prominently used among ancient Celts and pagans. It symbolizes the Goddess and is associated with life, death, and rebirth. The Sacred Spiral also represents the movement of celestial objects in the sky and the everlasting nature of things.

The Sun Wheel

The Sun Cross, or the Sun Wheel, is a pagan symbol that symbolizes the sun. It represents lids, immortality, fertility, and life-granting forces. The Sun Wheel also depicts the Eight Sabbats of Wicca and the four seasons of the year.

The Tree of Life

This symbol carries great meaning for several ancient civilizations, including that of the Celts. Accordig to Norse Mythology, this ash tree was thought to serve as a bridge for the Nine Realms. Trees and nature, in general, are very important to Celtic practitioners, which is why tribes chose to settle near trees and meet under them.

The Triple Horn of Odin

Trinities are highly pronounced in pagan traditions, and the Triple Horn of Odin is no exception. This symbol, which is also known as the horned triskele, is made up of three horns joined together to create what looks like a triangle. It is believed to illustrate the 3 times that Odin, the god of war and death, drank the mystical wisdom and poetry mead, which was thought to be made of the blood of a wise god. Horns were mentioned several times in the Manuscripts of the Prose Edda, and Vikings typically used them to toast in ceremonies, as well. These are all things that make this symbol particularly significant to the pagan faith.

Water

Water is an important symbol used in pagan invocation practices and rituals. The alchemical symbol of water is the exact opposite of that of fire: an inverted triangle. The pagan symbol for water is associated with femininity and is representative of the womb. It is commonly used in love rituals, as well as purification and cleansing ones.

Conclusion

As one of the oldest religions in the world, Paganism has an incredibly rich history. Learning about its background and evolution can be a great stepping stone if you want to develop any type of Pagan practice. This book has introduced you to the lives of the ancient Pagans - including their beliefs and their fight to maintain them when pressured by other religions. You've also learned that Paganism encompasses a wide range of practices and has once dominated the beliefs of the entire world's population. While nowadays it is less commonly practiced, anyone can embrace the Pagan path, regardless of their cultural or religious background.

Paganism is a spirituality-based religion, an aspect that helps followers understand and develop their practices. At the core of the belief system is a reverence for several gods and goddesses, all believed to impact a certain aspect of life. The deities are also linked to natural elements, which is in accordance with the other crucial dogma in Paganism - the veneration of nature. Nature and the gods are celebrated through different festivities like the equinoxes, representing a significant turning point in nature and people's lives.

Contemporary practices have held onto some of the ancient traditions, although some only in a very rudimentary form. Others have incorporated elements from other religions mainly due to the pressure of assimilation and survival. Neopaganism and Wicca (one of the newest Pagan religions) are both inspired by ancient magic practices. The latter represents an entirely new form of the spiritual path. If you feel that this path answers your spiritual needs, the chapter about its practical use can help you implement it into your practices.

The form of Paganism you've learned about in this book is Norse Paganism. While Wiccans rely on magical practices to reach spiritual goals, Norse Pagans have a high reverence for the afterlife and their ancestors. In Norse beliefs, ancestors are considered to be just as powerful guides as the deities are. Modern Norse Pagan practices incorporate rites of passage, festivals, and plenty of other acts you can perform - just as those who walked the old Norse Seidrs path did. These ancient shamanic practitioners were the masters of journeying and trance, through which they accessed all kinds of information.

The most common way to access information is through the Norse runes. Apart from being the letters of an ancient alphabet, runes are also unique divinatory tools with magical powers that reveal future events. The runes are divided into three major groups called Aetts - which hold the key to a specific set of information in the practitioner's subconscious. Their use requires learning about their symbolism but also highly developed intuitive skills.

Last but not least, you've learned about the connection between Celtic Shamanism and Druidry - two practices that, in ancient times, were held in high regard. Both Shamans and Druids were highly trusted members of Celtic societies. Yet nowadays, their roles have taken a divergent path through history. While shamans retained their healing practices, druids started to veer towards the patronage of arts, history, and philosophy. Despite this, Druids remain one of the most mysterious practitioners of Paganism. However, as you've learned from the book, if you choose to walk the Druid path, there are plenty of ways to do it.

Here's another book by Silvia Hill that you might like

Free Bonus from Silvia Hill available for limited time

Hi Spirituality Lovers!

My name is Silvia Hill, and first off, I want to THANK YOU for reading my book.

Now you have a chance to join my exclusive spirituality email list so you can get the ebooks below for free as well as the potential to get more spirituality ebooks for free! Simply click the link below to join.

P.S. Remember that it's 100% free to join the list.

~~$27~~ FREE BONUSES

- 9 Types of Spirit Guides and How to Connect to Them
- How to Develop Your Intuition: 7 Secrets for Psychic Development and Tarot Reading
- Tarot Reading Secrets for Love, Career, and General Messages

Access your free bonuses here
https://livetolearn.lpages.co/paganism-for-beginners-paperback/

References

What is Paganism? (2011, December 17). Pagan Federation International. https://www.paganfederation.org/what-is-paganism/

Hertzenberg, S., & Hertzenberg, S. (n.d.). What Are the Different Pagan Religions? Beliefnet.Com. https://www.beliefnet.com/faiths/pagan-and-earth-based/what-are-the-different-pagan-religions.aspx

Buker, R. (2018). Samhain. Piscataqua Press.

Celebrating the ancient Egyptian new year. (n.d.). Gov.Eg. https://egymonuments.gov.eg/events/celebrating-the-ancient-egyptian-new-year/

Colagrossi, M. (2018, November 27). 10 of the greatest ancient and pagan holidays. Big Think. https://bigthink.com/the-past/pagan-holidays/

Dowdey, S. (2007, December 5). How reincarnation works. HowStuffWorks. https://people.howstuffworks.com/reincarnation.htm

EarthSpirit. (2017, April 14). Paganism and Myths of Creation. EarthSpirit; EarthSpirit Inc. http://www.earthspirit.com/paganism-myths-creation

Kershaw, D. (2022, June 8). Pagan gods from across the ancient world. History Cooperative; The History Cooperative. https://historycooperative.org/pagan-gods/

Land, G. (n.d.). The 12 gods and goddesses of pagan Rome. History Hit. https://www.historyhit.com/the-gods-and-goddesses-of-pagan-rome/

Mark, J. J. (2016). Egyptian afterlife - the field of reeds. World History Encyclopedia. https://www.worldhistory.org/article/877/egyptian-afterlife---the-field-of-reeds/

Pagan beliefs. (n.d.). https://www.bbc.co.uk/religion/religions/paganism/beliefs/beliefs.shtml

Paganism. (n.d.). Nhs.uk. http://www.waht.nhs.uk/en-GB/NHS-Mobile/Our-Services/?depth=4&srcid=2007

Ravenwood, C. (2021). Celebrating samhain: A coloring and activity book. Independently Published.

S., J. (2019, June 3). Norse afterlife. Norse and Viking Mythology; vkngjewelry. https://blog.vkngjewelry.com/en/norse-afterlife/

Sogani, G. (2022, February 6). Religion and gods in the ancient pagan world. Wondrium Daily. https://www.wondriumdaily.com/religion-and-gods-in-the-ancient-pagan-world/

The Current Chief, The Former Chief, & Patroness, O. (2019, December 15). Samhain - rituals & traditions. Order of Bards, Ovates & Druids; OBOD. https://druidry.org/druid-way/teaching-and-practice/druid-festivals/samhain-festival

The Hell of ancient Egypt. (n.d.). Touregypt.net. http://www.touregypt.net/featurestories/hell.htm

Tomlin, A. (2022, May 18). Norse gods, goddesses and giants: the ultimate list. Routes North. https://www.routesnorth.com/language-and-culture/norse-gods-goddesses-and-giants/

What is Yule? (n.d.). Almanac.com. https://www.almanac.com/content/what-yule-log-christmas-traditions

Wigington, P. (2013, March 25). What do Pagans believe about the creation of the world? Learn Religions. https://www.learnreligions.com/pagans-and-creation-stories-2561497

Wigington, P. (2019, March 28). Norse deities. Learn Religions. https://www.learnreligions.com/norse-deities-4590158

John Halstead, C. (2015, October 2). We're Not All Witches: An Introduction to Neo-Paganism. HuffPost

Magick, B. B. (2018, December 13). Witchcraft, Wicca, and Paganism - What's the Difference? Blessed Be Magick. https://blessedbemagick.com/blogs/news/witchcraft-wicca-and-paganism-what-s-the-difference

Stonestreet, J., Leander, K., & Rivera, R. (2020, February 4). Wicca and Eclectic Neo-Paganism: Beliefs and Practices, Emerging Worldviews 22. Breakpoint. https://ec2-52-34-39-89.us-west-2.compute.amazonaws.com/wicca-and-eclectic-neo-paganism-beliefs-and-practices-emerging-worldviews-22/

Bradley, C. (2020, December 23). "Pagan" vs. "Wicca": What Is The

Difference? Dictionary.Com. https://www.dictionary.com/e/pagan-vs-wicca-pagan-vs-heathen/

We'Moon. (n.d.). Understanding Altars: What is an altar, and how to bring altar magic into my life. We'Moon. https://wemoon.ws/blogs/magical-arts/understanding-altars-what-is-an-altar-and-how-to-bring-altar-magic-into-my-life

Wigington, P. (n.d.). 9 Things to Include in Your Book of Shadows. Learn Religions. https://www.learnreligions.com/make-a-book-of-shadows-2562826

Blake, D. (2021, September 16). 10 Easy Ways to Create a Book of Shadows or Make an Existing Book Your Own. Llewellyn Worldwide. https://www.llewellyn.com/journal/article/2942

Vamvoukakis, A. (2022, July 11). How to Cast a Circle for Wiccans and Witches. The Embroidered Forest. https://theembroideredforest.com/blogs/wicca/how-to-cast-a-circle

Chatterjee, A. (2021, October 30). Be a modern witch with 7 daily spells and rituals that attract positivity. Tweak India. https://tweakindia.com/culture/discover/modern-witch-share-7-daily-practices-to-attract-good-vibes-only/

Siedlak, M. J. (2016). Wiccan Spells: Mojo's Wiccan Series. Createspace Independent Publishing Platform.

Dan. (2012, November 14). Norse mythology for Smart People - the ultimate online guide to Norse mythology and religion. Norse Mythology for Smart People. https://norse-mythology.org/

Norman. (2009, February 14). The origins of the Norse mythology. The Norse Gods; Norman. https://thenorsegods.com/the-origins-of-the-norse-mythology/

The faith. (n.d.). Asatru UK. https://www.asatruuk.org/the-faith

The old Nordic religion today. (n.d.). National Museum of Denmark. https://en.natmus.dk/historical-knowledge/denmark/prehistoric-period-until-1050-ad/the-viking-age/religion-magic-death-and-rituals/the-old-nordic-religion-today/

Time Nomads. (2021, June 20). Norse Paganism for beginners: Quick introduction + resources. Time Nomads | Your Pagan Store Online; Time Nomads. https://www.timenomads.com/norse-paganism-for-beginners/

Wigington, P. (2019, March 28). Norse deities. Learn Religions. https://www.learnreligions.com/norse-deities-4590158

Aletheia. (2018, October 22). How to induce a trance state for deep psychospiritual work ★ LonerWolf. LonerWolf.

Dan. (2012, November 15). Seidr. Norse Mythology for Smart People. https://norse-mythology.org/concepts/seidr/

Greenberg, M. (2020, November 16). Seidr magic in viking culture. MythologySource; Mike Greenberg, PhD. https://mythologysource.com/seidr-magic-viking-culture/

Skjalden. (2018, March 11). Völva the viking witch or seeress. Nordic Culture. https://skjalden.com/volva-the-viking-witch-or-seeress/

Wright, M. S. (2015, March 3). Wicca for beginners: Visualizations for grounding and centering meditations. Exemplore. https://exemplore.com/wicca-witchcraft/Wicca-for-Beginners-Visualizations-for-Grounding-and-Centering-Meditations

Dan. (2012, November 14). Runes. Norse Mythology for Smart People. https://norse-mythology.org/runes/

Anne C. Sørensen, R. M. J. H. (n.d.). Runes. Vikingeskibsmuseet i Roskilde. https://www.vikingeskibsmuseet.dk/en/professions/education/viking-age-people/runes

Dan. (2013, June 29). The Origins of the Runes. Norse Mythology for Smart People. https://norse-mythology.org/runes/the-origins-of-the-runes/

Dan. (2013, June 29). Runic Philosophy and Magic. Norse Mythology for Smart People. https://norse-mythology.org/runes/runic-philosophy-and-magic/

Dan. (2013, June 29). The Meanings of the Runes. Norse Mythology for Smart People. https://norse-mythology.org/runes/the-meanings-of-the-runes/

Shelley, A. (2022, February 22). Futhark Runes: Symbols, Meanings and How to Use Them. Andrea Shelley Designs. https://andreashelley.com/blog/futhark-runes-symbols-and-meanings/

Sam, T. +., & Wander, T. (2020, November 25). Rune Meanings And How To Use Rune Stones For Divination —. Two Wander x Elysium Rituals. https://www.twowander.com/blog/rune-meanings-how-to-use-runestones-for-divination

Sam, T. +., & Wander, T. (2020, November 25). Rune Meanings And How To Use Rune Stones For Divination —. Two Wander x Elysium Rituals. https://www.twowander.com/blog/rune-meanings-how-to-use-runestones-for-divination

AstroMundus, & Happy, happy.com. pt. (2021, November 18). Runes and Their Meanings • . AstroMundus. https://astromundus.com/en/runes-meanings/

Wigington, P. (n.d.). What Is Rune Casting? Origins and Techniques. Learn Religions. https://www.learnreligions.com/rune-casting-4783609

Jessica, S. (2021, April 27). How to Read Rune Stones. Norse and Viking Mythology. https://blog.vkngjewelry.com/en/rune-divination-how-to-read-the-runes/

I. E. (IrishMyths.com). (2022, April 12). Who were the druids? Demystifying the mystics of the ancient Celtic world. Irish Myths. https://irishmyths.com/2022/04/11/what-are-druids/

Spaeth, M. J. D. (2020). Celtic Shamanism. In Encyclopedia of Psychology and Religion (pp. 370–372). Springer International Publishing.

Terravara. (2021, April 23). Shamanism vs druidism: What's the difference? Terravara. https://www.terravara.com/shamanism-vs-druidism/

The Current Chief, The Former Chief, & Patroness, O. (2019a, November 27). Bard. Order of Bards, Ovates & Druids; OBOD. https://druidry.org/druid-way/what-druidry/what-is-a-bard

The Current Chief, The Former Chief, & Patroness, O. (2019b, November 27). Ovate. Order of Bards, Ovates & Druids; OBOD. https://druidry.org/druid-way/what-druidry/what-is-an-ovate

The Current Chief, The Former Chief, & Patroness, O. (2019c, November 27). What is druidry? Order of Bards, Ovates & Druids; OBOD. https://druidry.org/druid-way/what-druidry

The Editors of Encyclopedia Britannica. (2022). Druid. In Encyclopedia Britannica.

The sacred fire - Celtic shamanism. (n.d.). Sacredfire.net. https://www.sacredfire.net/shaman.html

Who were the Druids? (2017, March 21). Historic UK. https://www.historic-uk.com/HistoryUK/HistoryofWales/Druids/

Wigington, P. (2007, May 23). Who are today's Druids? Learn Religions. https://www.learnreligions.com/about-druidism-druidry-2562546

An Introduction to the Basics of Modern Druid practice. (2017, January 29). The Druid Network. https://druidnetwork.org/what-is-druidry/learning-resources/shaping-the-wheel/introduction-basics-modern-druid-practice/

Damh the Bard. (2015, July 24). Druidry for beginners - where to start? The senses. Damh the Bard. https://www.paganmusic.co.uk/druidry-for-beginners-where-to-start-the-senses/

Ede-Weaving, M. (2021, April 22). Awen. Order of Bards, Ovates & Druids. https://druidry.org/resources/awen

How does one become a Druid? (2013, March 10). The Druid Network. https://druidnetwork.org/what-is-druidry/beliefs-and-definitions/articles/how-does-one-become-a-druid/

Hertzenberg, S., & Hertzenberg, S. (n.d.). What Are the Different Pagan Religions? Beliefnet.Com. https://www.beliefnet.com/faiths/pagan-and-earth-based/what-are-the-different-pagan-religions.aspx

Pagan paths. (n.d.). https://www.bbc.co.uk/religion/religions/paganism/subdivisions/paths.shtml

Printed in Great Britain
by Amazon

31453821R10073